Thomas Stratton

The Affinity Between the Hebrew Language and the Celtic

Being a comparison between Hebrew and the Gaelic language, or the Celtic of

Scotland

Thomas Stratton

The Affinity Between the Hebrew Language and the Celtic
Being a comparison between Hebrew and the Gaelic language, or the Celtic of Scotland

ISBN/EAN: 9783743414686

Manufactured in Europe, USA, Canada, Australia, Japa

Cover: Foto ©Lupo / pixelio.de

Manufactured and distributed by brebook publishing software (www.brebook.com)

Thomas Stratton

The Affinity Between the Hebrew Language and the Celtic

THE AFFINITY

BETWEEN

THE HEBREW LANGUAGE

AND

THE CELTIC:

BEING

A COMPARISON BETWEEN HEBREW AND THE GAELIC LANGUAGE,

OR THE CELTIC OF SCOTLAND.

BY

THOMAS STRATTON, M.D. Edin.,

R. N.

THIRD EDITION.

EDINBURGH:

MACLACHAN AND STEWART, SOUTH BRIDGE.
LONDON: SIMPKIN, MARSHALL, AND CO.
PLYMOUTH: W. BRENDON AND SON.

1872.

Price Two Shillings.

THE AFFINITY

BETWEEN

THE HEBREW LANGUAGE

AND

THE CELTIC:

BEING

A COMPARISON BETWEEN HEBREW AND THE GAELIC LANGUAGE,

OR THE CELTIC OF SCOTLAND.

BY

THOMAS STRATTON, M.D. Edin.,

Dep. Inspector-Gen., R. N.

THIRD EDITION.

EDINBURGH:

MACLACHLAN AND STEWART, SOUTH BRIDGE.

LONDON: SIMPKIN, MARSHALL, AND CO.

PLYMOUTH: W. BRENDON AND SON.

1872.

SIR ALEXANDER ARMSTRONG, K.C.B.,

M.D. Edin.,

HONORARY PHYSICIAN TO THE QUEEN,

DIRECTOR-GENERAL OF THE MEDICAL DEPARTMENT OF
THE NAVY.

SIR,

As that branch of Medicine called Physiology includes an account of the different races of mankind, and as a description of the various divisions of the human family has to be illustrated chiefly by referring to the languages spoken by them, there is some reason for saying that the affinity of languages is a subject within the wide area of Medical Inquiry.

In 1833 I drew up a short Comparative Vocabulary of Hebrew and Gaelic. In 1840 this was printed at the end of my Comparative Vocabulary of Greek and Gaelic. In 1870 it was reprinted without any alteration. After 1833 or 1840 I did not look into the subject again till November, 1871, when, after a few days, I made the discovery that by taking away the first part of many Hebrew words the next syllable, or the next two syllables, resembled in sound and meaning a word in Gaelic. The words which, treated in this way, give this result number about four hundred and fifty.

At first I intended waiting till I had time to re-arrange the matter of my other essays relating to Gaelic (*Celtic Origin of Greek and Latin and of Classical Proper Names*), but on second thoughts, it seemed to me that the subject was of so much interest and novelty, that the Essay was worthy of being published at once, and also of being inscribed to one who, some years ago, was selected to be the Head of an important Department of the Public Service.

I am, Sir, your obedient Servant,

THOMAS STRATTON, M.D.,

R.N.

May, 1872.

PREFACE.

Of those who may take up this short Essay relating to Gaelic, it occurs to me that some may wish to know what local opportunities the writer has had of being practically acquainted with that language.

As, every ten or twenty years, the number of those who speak Gaelic is somewhat less, it is as well to make some reference to dates.

Although it is said that egotism should be avoided, let me mention that, born in the town of Perth (1816), I remained there for about eight years.

I then lived, for about five years, fifteen miles north-west from Perth, at Dunkeld, which is on the Gaelic border, and has been called the mouth of the Highlands. Being the mouth of the Highlands, it has been said of it that it ought to speak Gaelic. Every day I heard a good deal of Gaelic spoken, but I did not pay any attention to it.

The next four years, from 1829 to 1833, I spent in Northumberland. In 1831 a strong feeling of nationality—which I have always had on all subjects—took the particular bent of a wish to learn Gaelic. At the age of fifteen I procured Stewart's *Gaelic Grammar*, Macleod and Dewar's *Gaelic Dictionary*, and a few other books; and in the course of two or three months, without any help, taught myself the language.

The next four years, from November, 1833, to August, 1837, I was in Scotland, attending medical classes at college, and had no time for any except professional studies.

In July, 1840, the *Affinity of Latin to the Celtic* was published; in September, 1840, the *Celtic Origin of Greek* (at the end of this was given a short Comparative Vocabulary of Hebrew and Gaelic); and, in 1845, the *Celtic Origin of Classical Proper Names.*

In 1870 a second edition was issued of all the above.

I have been about twenty-six years in full-pay in the Navy, of which about ten years in different parts of Canada, and after that about ten years and a half in Prince Edward Island, near Nova Scotia—in the winter at Prince Edward Island, and in the summer about

Cape Breton, Nova Scotia, Newfoundland, &c. In various localities in Nova Scotia, Cape Breton, and Prince Edward Island, there is a good deal of Gaelic spoken; but I was not in these particular districts. For eighteen years (1849 to 1867) I was not once in Scotland. To Dunkeld and its vicinity four or five visits of a few weeks each have of late been all the opportunity I have had of hearing Gaelic spoken.

As to the area over which Gaelic is or has been spoken, and the degree of its use therein, some information may be found in the three following publications:—

The *Statistical Account of Scotland*, in twenty-one volumes, published between 1791 and 1799, was drawn up from the communications of the ministers of the different parishes.

The *New Statistical Account of Scotland*, in fifteen volumes, octavo, published about 1847. This is on a better plan than the former, as each county is in a separate volume, and may be purchased separately.

For a great many years Messrs. Oliver and Boyd have published the *Edinburgh Almanac*, a yearly volume containing copious information on most subjects relating to Scotland: it notes the churches where the service is either wholly or partially in Gaelic. The year 1815 was the one when it began to denote this. It is to be hoped that it will ever continue to do so.

Every time that the decennial census is taken, it would be very desirable in the Highlands and Hebrides to ascertain—1. The number of persons who speak Gaelic only. 2 Number who speak Gaelic and English. 3. Total number speaking Gaelic. 4. Number able to read Gaelic. 5. Proportion per cent. of Gaelic-speaking persons, and the total population of each parish and county. These few columns being added to the tables would not be much additional trouble to the enumerators. It was in 1801 that they began the regular system of taking the census every ten years. Foreigners will hardly believe that a matter so important and interesting has always been neglected. During the year 1870, from various bodies and individuals, letters were sent urging that the results of the census of 1871 should contain this information; but Highlanders and enthusiastic Gaelic scholars were again disappointed. If at each census these language-statistics were ascertained and published, they would in after times be looked upon as a valuable historical record. It is very sad that the census of 1871 should have this defect or omission: perhaps the General Assembly of the Church of Scotland might request the minister of each parish in the Highlands and Hebrides to draw up the number of the Gaelic-speaking inhabitants, &c.

The same steps ought to be taken at each census in Ireland, Wales, and the Isle of Man. In Wales the matter was always neglected till 1871. In the Isle of Man it has always been neglected. In Ireland it was neglected till 1851. In that year it was taken, and also in 1861, and, I suppose, in 1871. They who manage the census in Ireland deserve great credit for what they have done, and they make Ireland contrast most favourably with the other Celtic-speaking parts of the United Kingdom.

I do not make the slightest pretence of being a Hebrew scholar; in the case of nine or ten words, perhaps some who are Hebrew scholars may see that these might more correctly be referred to other words in Hebrew, instead of trying to find distant cousins for them in Celtic.

It is unnecessary to observe, that the plan of cutting off the first part of Hebrew words may be used for the purpose of comparing Hebrew with other tongues besides the Celtic.

As possibly these pages may be again printed, I shall be glad to receive, addressed to myself, any corrections or suggestions that may occur to my readers.

Any published criticisms, good-natured or otherwise, will be carefully attended to.

4, Valletort Terrace,
  Stoke,
  Devonport,
  May, 1872.

THE AFFINITY

BETWEEN

THE HEBREW AND THE CELTIC.

EARLY in the year 1833 I drew up a short Comparative Vocabulary of Hebrew and Gaelic. In 1840 this was printed at the end of my Comparative Greek and Gaelic Vocabulary. In 1870 this was reprinted without any alteration. After 1833 or 1840 I did not look into the subject again till November, 1871, when I made many additions to my former list. On this occasion (1872) the manner of spelling Hebrew words in English letters, is the one followed by Aaron Pick in that work of great ability and industry, *The Bible-Student's Concordance.* (London: Hamilton, Adams & Co. 1845. Pp. 590.)

In comparing one language with another, there are two questions to be considered; first, the grammar of the two languages; and, secondly, the separate words of each.

In Hebrew the prepositions are incorporated with the personal pronouns; the same is done in Gaelic: aig (at) and other fifteen prepositions are incorporated with the personal pronouns. This was pointed out by Stewart in his *Gaelic Grammar.* (Edinburgh, 1801; and second edition, 1812, page 129.)

Of Hebrew nouns a plural termination is *im* or *eem ;* this is like the Gaelic Mo, *more.*

After 1833 or 1840 I did not look into the subject again till November, 1871. After a few days I made a discovery that gave me a key to word-analogies I had not previously noticed. I found that, after taking away the first part of a Hebrew word, the next syllable, or the next two syllables, resembled a word in Gaelic. In this word-dissection there is taken away either—

1. An initial vowel, or
2. An initial vowel-sound, or
3. An initial consonant, or
4. An initial consonant followed by a vowel-sound.

There are about four hundred and fifty-two Hebrew words which, after being treated in this way, are like Gaelic words. Under the letter aleph, there are thirty-nine words; under beth, eight; under gimel, fourteen; under daleth, twelve; under he, fifteen; under vov, none; under zain, nineteen; under kheth, twenty-seven; under teth, five; under yod, twenty-nine; under kaph, thirteen; under lamed, ten; under mem, sixty-one; under nun, forty-three; under zamech, twenty-eight; under ayin, twenty-two; under pe, six; under tsade (*ts* prefixed), fourteen; under tsade (*t* prefixed), six; under koph, fifteen; under resh, two; under shin or sin, fifty-nine; and under the letter tov, fifteen words.

As the prefixing of a vowel, or of a vowel-sound, is not as distinct as the prefixing of a consonant, I show separately the number of words (having a prefix) beginning with—aleph, thirty-nine words; he, fifteen; yod, twenty-nine; ayin, twenty-two; in all one hundred and five; leaving three hundred and forty-seven words beginning with a prefixed consonant. It saves repetition to speak of the *Hebrew prefixing* without always adding *or the Gaelic omitting*.

In the following pages there are given about twelve hundred and seventy Hebrew words, which in meaning and sound are like words in Gaelic. This is four hundred and fifty-two words having a non-Celtic prefix, and eight hundred and twenty other words.

I have not reckoned the whole number of words in Hebrew (to be found in the Hebrew Old Testament); it is only a random guess that the twelve hundred and seventy Hebrew words akin to Gaelic are perhaps about one-fourth, or it may be one-third, of all the words in the Hebrew language.

In 1833 I noted several words with a syllable prefixed; so that I was then nearly making the discovery which I did not make till 1871. In 1833 I gave but a very cursory attention to the subject, being then about to attend medical classes.

In this comparison of Hebrew with the Celtic, only one branch of the Celtic is referred to; namely, the Gaelic, now spoken in the Highlands and Western Isles of Scotland. The words quoted may be found in the *Gaelic Dictionary* by Macleod and Dewar. (Glasgow, 1831; and, second edition, Edinburgh, 1833.) Any remarks here about the Gaelic or Scoto-Celtic apply equally to the Irish language, and to the Manx. By referring to the Welsh, Cornish, or Armoric, it is likely that other proofs of Hebrew-Celtic linguistic kinship would be found, as words which one Celtic dialect may have lost may be preserved in another; and words now in use in one dialect may be capable of being referred to roots extant only in another.

A derivation or a case of word-affinity is sometimes like a riddle: it is very easy *after it is explained*.

The Celtic language has never received the attention its antiquity and importance merit. Ignorance of Celtic has always characterised nearly the whole of the Greek and Latin scholars of Great Britain and Ireland: this ignorance dates so far back that it may be called traditional.* I fancy the same remark may be made respecting the Hebrew scholars of the United Kingdom. Some writers pass over the subject of early languages without any reference to the Celtic; and others seem unwilling to admit its rights, its just and reasonable claims to consideration. When they come to speak of the Celtic, from what they say, it is clear that names, some of considerable learning, some of great learning, have not been able to extricate their minds from the prejudices in which they were brought up.

The reader unacquainted with Gaelic is requested to notice that *bh* and *mh* are sounded like the English *v; ph* like *f: c* and *g* are always hard like *k*. On some occasions *cn* and *gn* are sounded *cr* and *gr*. At the end of a word *ch* is like *ch* in *loch*, as the Scotch pronounce it; *d* and *t* when followed by *h* are generally silent: in some cases *d* and *t* are retained because formerly they were sounded; and *h* is added to show that now they are not pronounced. These few remarks are sufficient for the purpose of derivation or word-comparison: more minute rules are to be found in Stewart's *Gaelic Grammar*, and in Macalpine's *Gaelic Pronouncing Dictionary*.

In the case of the words when at the beginning of the word a syllable is either added in Hebrew or omitted in Gaelic, a hyphen is occasionally used in an arbitrary way, that the theory offered for the consideration of the reader may catch the eye more readily: it would have been more complete to have used the hyphen in all the cases. The Hebrew words are given first in the line, and in small capitals; the Gaelic words are given in Roman letters.

---

* There is no allusion here to the ministers of parishes in the Highlands and Hebrides, or other clergymen who have occasion to use Gaelic in their churches.

ALEPH.

Aleph, the first Hebrew letter. The first Gaelic letter is called Ailm, *the elm*.

Some Hebrew and Gaelic words are alike in meaning and sound, except that either the Hebrew prefixes a vowel-sound, or the Gaelic omits an initial vowel: of this there are about thirty-eight instances.

A conjectural affinity is offered for the consideration of the reader: some Hebrew and Gaelic words are alike in meaning and sound, except that an initial consonant is either omitted in Hebrew, or added in Gaelic.

FIRST GROUP.

Hebrew words beginning with a vowel, or a vowel-sound, and Gaelic words beginning with a vowel:

AIL, *God ;* compare with Gaelic Ailt, *high.*

AIL, *mighty ;* ELOUHEEM, *superior ;* ALIYOH, *an upper room ;* AL, *upon ;* AIL, *an arch over a door :* Ailt, *high.*

ALOUPH, *a head, a chief :* Alp, *high.*

ARMOUN, *a royal citadel :* Ard, *high ;* monadh, *a hill.*

ARGOZ, *a coffer, a box :* Airc, *a chest.*

OMAIN, *amen, so be it :* Amhuil, amh-uil, *like.*

OMAR, OMOR, *say :* Abair, *say.*

OV, AV, *a father, ancestor :* Ab (obs.), *a father.*

AID, *mist :* Ad (obs.), *water ;* or dubh, *dark.*

OKHUZ, *possession :* Aig, *in possession.*

AKH, *but :* Ach, *but.*

AMEETH, *an associate :* Amhuil, amh-uil, *like ;* or comh, *together ;* c omitted.

APHEEK, *a stream :* Abh, *water.*

AOOM, *a pond :* ag like *aig* in Aigeal, *a pool,* and aigeann, *a pool.*

AKZOR, *cruel :* Aiccar, *cruel.*

ELEEL, *an idol ;* AILEEM, *images :* like the second syllable of Amhuil, amh-uil, *like.*

OOR, *to lighten, to illuminate ;* OUR, OOR, *light :* Ear, *the east* (break of day); also like brath, *fire ;* b omitted.

OOKHEEM, *howling animals :* Eigh, *a cry.*

EE, *an island :* I, *an island.*

OLAKH, *corrupted :* Olc, *wicked.*

OLAPH, *to teach :* Ollamh, *a learned person.*

OTHOH, *to come:* Uidhe, *a step, a journey.*

OKH, *alas;* EE, *mourning:* Och, *alas.* Gaelic is very partial to the sound *ch* at the end of a word when apparently it might be dispensed with, as tula, *a hill,* which also appears in the form tulach.

UMLAL, *to languish:* Umhal, *meek.*

ESHED, *a torrent:* esh like Uisge, uis-ge, *water.*

AREETH (Chaldee), *earth;* ERETS, ARTSOUTH, *land, earth, country:* Uir, *earth.* Also like the Gaelic ruadh, *red.* The Gaelic word for earth is akin to the word for redness. See under adomoh.

AKHAR, *after;* AKHOURAI, *the hinder parts;* AKHOURANEETH, *back again;* AKHAREETH, *latter, last;* AKHAIR, *another,* from AKHAR, *after:* Iar, *after;* kh prefixed; and then *a* prefixed.

OVAV, *unripe:* Amh, *crude, raw.*

SECOND GROUP.

Either a vowel-sound prefixed in Hebrew, or an initial vowel omitted in Gaelic.

ABBEER, *mighty:* ABEER, a-beer, *might,* like the Gaelic Mor, *great.*

APH, *anger;* AIVOH, *enmity:* Fuath, *hatred.*

AIPHER, *ashes:* Brath, *fire.*

AIPHAILOH, *thick darkness:* Feile, *a covering.*

AD, *to, unto:* Do, *to.*

AIN, *not;* AYIN, *not;* OYIN, *not:* Neo, *not.*

ATTOH, *thou:* Du, *thou.*

ASHAIR, *to arrange:* Sreath, *a row.*

AGVOH, *affection;* the *gv* like Caomh, *beloved.*

AITHON, *stubborn, irresistible:* Dian, *vehement, violent.*

AYIL, *a stone side-post:* perhaps like Lia, *a stone.*

AGOL, *a round drop* (see under Gol): Calbh, *a head;* the idea is something round.

EGROUPH, *a fist:* Cior (obs.), *a hand.*

EVROH, *wrath:* Fearg, *anger.*

IDRAI (Chaldee), *an earthen floor:* Tir, *earth.*

OVOD, *lose:* Bho, *from* (the preposition turned into a verb).

ODOUN, *a lord, a master:* Tanaiste, tan-aiste, *a lord, a thane.*

OPHOH, *to bake:* Biadh, *food.*

OMEER, *foliage:* Barr, *the top* (say of a tree).

OGAV, *to fall in love with:* Caomh, *beloved.*

OUV, *a spirit of divination;* v like Faidh, *a prophet;* ou prefixed.

OVAIL, *waste ground:* Falamh, *empty;* hence the word fallow.

ORAKH, *to lengthen;* EREKH, *long:* Ruig, *extend.*

OKHAL, *to devour, eat up:* perhaps akin to Caol, *narrow* (whence perhaps a name for the gullet).

OUPHEL, *thick darkness:* Feile, *a covering.*

ASHOOR, *a course, an open space:* Srath, *a valley through which a river runs,* any low-lying country along a river, a strath, as Strathtay, &c.

IKKAR, *a ploughman;* kar like Gearr, *cut;* cut through the ground.

OKHAIN, *surely so;* akin to Hebrew KOON, *to fix, to erect;* KAN, *a basis, a pedestal;* KONAS, KONASH, *to gather into a place of security* (under the letter kaph): under the letter koph, see KAN, *a nest;* KONAN, *to make a nest:* under the letter kheth, see KHONOH, *to encamp;* under the letter shin, see SHEKHAN, *a resting-place:* also see MAKHANEH, *a camp;* MEKHOUNOH, *a foundation;* GAN, *a garden;* GONAN, *to enclose;* TEKHOUNOH, *establishment, estate, property;* NOKHOUN, *certain, fixed;* HOKAIN, *established.* All these Hebrew words are akin to each other, and to the Gaelic Comhnuidh, comhn-uidh, *a dwelling:* an comhnuidh, *continually.*

EMOUNOH, e-moun-oh, *firm;* AIMUN, ai-mun, *faith, belief, truth:* Bun. *foundation; b* to *m.*

OGAR, *to lay up a store,* as of provisions: Cuir, *set, place;* or Cro, *a hut, a house, an enclosure.*

EREZ, *cedar, a red wood:* perhaps akin to Ruadh, *red.*

AGARTOL (Chaldee), *a basin,* a-gar-tol: Cro, *anything round.*

AID, *calamity; d* like Dith, *want, destruction; ai* prefixed.

EVEN, *a stone:* perhaps akin to Ban, *white.* In Gaelic, lia is *a stone,* and lia, liath, is *grey:* the name for stones applied to the colour, or the name for the colour applied to stones.

AGERETH (Chaldee), *a letter:* Sgriob, *a line;* sgriobh, *write;* these two words from garbh, *rough.*

AIKH, *how:* Co, *who;* cia, *what; ai* prefixed.

AGOUDOH, *a bunch:* Cath, *a company.*

THIRD GROUP.

An initial consonant is either omitted in Hebrew, or added in Gaelic: this is a conjecture offered for the consideration of the reader. See the third group under the letter he, the third group under the letter ayin, and the second group under the letter yod.

OTHOH, *to become:* perhaps like Bi, bith, *to be; b* omitted.

ONIYOH, *a ship:* Long, *a ship; l* omitted.

OLOH, *to denounce:* Beul, *the mouth; b* omitted.

OLATS, *to compel:* Buail, *strike; b* omitted.

Oor, our, *light :* Brath, *a fire; b* omitted.

Oulom, *a porch :* perhaps like Beul, *mouth* (the mouth of the house); *b* omitted.

Osar, *to fetter :* perhaps like Cos, *a foot; c* omitted.

Onak, *to sigh :* Caoin, *lament; c* omitted.

Orat, *to lie in wait :* Crub, *crouch; c* omitted.

Ahavoh, *love;* ohav, *to love;* ivvoh, *to desire :* Caomh, *beloved; c* omitted.

Aniyoh, *suffering pain :* Caoin, *lament, groan; c* omitted.

Eelon (Chaldee), *a tree;* ailoun, *a grove of oaks :* Coille, *wood; c* omitted.

Onoosh, *helpless, feeble :* Faoin, *idle, unavailing; f* omitted.

Aits, *a tree, wood;* oe (Chaldee), *wood, timber;* oo (Syriac), *timber;* Fiodh, *wood; f* omitted.

Arbeh, ar-beh, *a grasshopper; ar* like Feur, *grass; f* omitted.

Ouhel, *a tent :* Feile, *a covering; f* omitted.

Aith, *a coulter;* ait, *an iron pen :* perhaps akin to Gath, *a dart,* &c. (the idea is *cutting*) ; *g* omitted.

Okh, *a brother;* akhouth, *a sister :* perhaps akin to Mac, *a son; m* omitted. A group who are brothers to each other, are the sons of one person; and a group of the sons of one man, are each other's brothers. In a very early state of society the ideas about relationship, and the names for it, were not very clear. See Sir John Lubbock's *Origin of Civilization,* 1870, page 50.

Aimoh, *dread :* Tioma, *afraid; t* omitted.

Aish, *fire;* aizaih (Syriac), *heat :* Teas, *heat; t* omitted.

Odom, *earthy, name of the first man* (Adam); adomoh, *red earth;* admoh, *earthy;* oudem, *a ruby;* perhaps *od* like Ruadh, *red; r* omitted.

Onoo, *we :* Sinn, *us; s* omitted.

Adai, *ever;* ad, *for ever :* Sith, *continually; s* omitted.

FOURTH GROUP.

Almonoh, al-monoh, *a widow :* perhaps like Mnaoi, *a woman.*

Albeen, *to be whiter :* Ban, *white.*

BETH.

Beth is the second Hebrew letter: there is an idea that it received its name from Beth or bayith, *a house,* representing a tent, the primitive house of early tribes, its form being like the shape of a tent. Hebrew Bayith, *a house,* is like Gaelic Buth, *a pavilion, booth ;*

Lowland-Scotch, *bothy*. The second Gaelic letter is called Beith, *the birch tree.*

Some Hebrew and Gaelic words are alike in meaning and sound, except that an initial *b* is either added in Hebrew or omitted in Gaelic; either *b*, or *b* followed by a vowel-sound.

Some Hebrew and Gaelic words are alike in meaning and sound, except that either the Hebrew omits an initial vowel-sound, or the Gaelic prefixes a vowel.

FIRST GROUP.

Words which begin with *b* in both languages.

BOASH, *to corrupt, to rot;* akin to Bas, *death.*

BEOUDEE, *existing :* Bith, *to be.*

BOLAK, *to lay waste :* Buail, *smite.*

BOLAG, *to stir up :* Buail, *strike.*

BAAL, *a master;* BOHAL, *to terrify;* BELYIAL, BELIAL, *a wicked person :* perhaps akin to Beal, *the god Belus, or Bel.*

BEN, *a structure, a building;* BONOH, *to build :* Bun, *a foundation.*

BAYITH, *a house :* Buth, *a tent, a pavilion, a bothy.*

BEEROH, *the residence of royalty :* BUTH, *a house;* righ, *a king.*

BETOUV, *in good spirits :* Buidheach, *well pleased.*

BAAR, *ignorant, stupid;* VAAR, *an ignorant man :* Borb, *savage.*

BOLA, *to swallow;* BOLEEL, *a mixture of fodder :* Beul, *the mouth.*

BOTSAIK, *dough;* bot like Biadh, *food.*

BEROUSH, *on, at the head of :* Barr, *top.*

BORO, *to create :* Beir, *to bring forth, to produce.*

BAR, *a son :* Bar (obs.), *a son,* like the Gaelic beir.

BEAIR, *a well, a cavity :* Bior (obs.), *a well, a fountain; water.*

BOUR, *a pit;* BOAR, *to clear away, to extirpate;* BERAIKHOH, *a pool of water :* Bior, also like bruid, *dig.*

BOAR, *to destroy :* Bruth, *bruise, crush;* or brath, *fire.*

BOUHEN, *a thumb;* akin to Bonn, *the sole of the foot.*

Compare with Latin penes, *in one's hand, or possession.* The Latin words penes, pinna, penna, sculponea (scul-ponea), and manus (here *b* to *m*) are akin to the Gaelic bonn. Speaking anatomically, hands (or arms and hands), feet (or legs and feet), wings, and fins, are the equivalents of each other.

BATH, *a measure of liquids :* Bath, *quench, drown.*

BAD, *a long branch, a pole :* Bat, *a staff.*

BITTOH, *to speak unadvisedly :* Baoth, *foolish.*

BORAKH, *to run :* Bruchd, *to rush forth.*

BASAM, *a spice; bas* like Bus, *the mouth.*

BEERONIYOUTH (Chaldee), *castles :* Barr, *a height ;* bearn, *a hill.*

VONOUTH, *daughters :* Bean, *a woman.*

VEAIN, *without :* Bho, *from.*

BOTSA, *to gain, to profit ;* BETSA, *gain, profit :* Buadh, *gain, success, victory.*

BEEPHES, *without measure ;* like Bho, *from ;* meas, *estimation.*

BOAIR, *a blaze, a flame ;* BIAIR, *to clear up, to consume ;* BOAR, *to blaze, to flame ;* BOHAR, *to brighten ;* BORAR, *to purify ;* BOROOR, *pure ;* BOROH, *pure ;* HAR, *pure ;* BORAK, *to glitter ;* VOOR, *purity ;* BOROK, *lightning ;* BOREKETH, *a glittering stone ;* BEREE, *brightness ;* BAHARETH, *a bright spot :* Brath, *fire.*

BOKHOH, *to bewail :* Beuc, *an outcry.*

BARZEL, *iron ;* perhaps from being prepared by fire : Brath, *fire.*

BOKHOUN, *a watch-tower :* Beachd, *vision ; oun* like dun (in composition un), *a hill.*

BAKOSHOH, *a petition,* hence BAKSHISH ; BIKHAISH, *to request :* Beuc, beuchd, *an outcry, a clamour* (beuc like focal, foc-al, *a word*).

<h2 style="text-align:center">SECOND GROUP.</h2>

An initial *b* is either added in Hebrew or omitted in Gaelic ; either *b*, or *b* followed by a vowel-sound.

BOKOR, bo-kor, *horned cattle ;* like Crodh, *cattle ;* also like bo, *an ox ;* corn, *a horn.*

BOKHAR, bo-khar, *to choose ;* perhaps like Cior (obs.), *the hand* (to take).

BIKHROH, b-ikh-roh, *a dromedary : ikh* like Each, *a horse ; roh* like ruith, *to run* (a swift horse).

BOLAM, bo-lam, *to restrain :* Lamh, *the hand* (suppose to hold).

BOU, *to come, to enter ;* BO, *to come :* Uidhe, *a step.*

BOO (Syriac), *to petition :* Eigh, *earnest entreaty.*

BOTSAR, b-ot-sar, *to heap up earth or stones :* At, *a swelling, a heap.*

BETEN, b-et-on, *the abdomen :* At, *a prominence.*

<h2 style="text-align:center">THIRD GROUP.</h2>

BEREETH, *a covenant ;* BIAIR, *to define :* Abair, *say ;* a omitted. The Gaelic bard, *a poet,* akin to abair.

BOROD, *hail :* Fuar, *cold ; f* to *b.*

BOZAZ, *to plunder ;* BOUZAIZ, *a plunderer :* Fas, *to lay waste ; f* to *b.*

BOGAD, *to be faithless,* bog-ad : Fag, *to leave ; f* to *b.*

BALOT, *wrapped up :* Fill, *fold ;* feile, *a covering ; f* to *b.*

BITTO, *to pronounce :* Faidh, *a prophet ; f* to *b.*

Beoud, *as long :* Fad, *long ;* f to b.

Beenoh, *understanding :* Mein, *mind ;* m to b.

Bain, *between :* Meadhon, *middle ;* m to b.

Bollal, *to mix, to confuse ;* boloh, *to wear out :* Meil, *grind ;* m to b.

Boosh, *shame :* Masladh, mas-ladh, *shame ;* m to b.

Booz, *contempt :* Masladh, *reproach ;* m to b.

Boos, *to tread upon ;* voos, *to tread upon :* like Greek pous, Latin pes, *a foot ;* like Gaelic Cos, *a foot ;* c to p.

GIMEL.

The third Hebrew letter. From a fancied resemblance to the figure of a camel, it is thought that this letter derived its name from Gomol, *a camel.* The Gaelic camal, *a camel,* is derived from cam, *crooked ;* al, *horse.*

Some Hebrew and Celtic words are alike in meaning and sound, except that either the Hebrew prefixes g, or the Celtic omits initial c or g ; either g, or g followed by a vowel-sound.

FIRST GROUP.

Words which begin with g in Hebrew, and with c or g in Gaelic.

Gan, *a garden ;* gonan, *to enclose, fence, protect.* Under the letter kheth, see khonoh, *to encamp :* under the letter kaph, see koon, *to erect ;* kan, *a basis :* konas, konash, *to gather into a place of security :* under the letter koph, see kan, *a nest :* konan, *to make a nest :* also see makhaneh, *a camp.* Of all these, the idea is an enclosure. Also see tekhounoh, *establishment, estate, property ;* tikhoun, *established :* shekhan, *a resting-place :* mekhounoh, *a foundation, a base.* All these Hebrew words are akin to each other, and to the Gaelic Comhnuidh, comhn-uidh, *a dwelling.*

Goor, *to dwell ;* gair, *a sojourner ;* gairooth, *a temporary dwelling :* Cro, *a hut, a cottage.*

Goor, *to frighten :* Crith, *shake with fear.*

Geres, *to grind :* Croc, *beat, pound.*

Goloh, *to discover, to reveal :* Glaodh, *to call* (also like sgeul, *a tale ;* s omitted).

Gooh, *to bellow :* Guth, *a voice.*

Goram, *to break to pieces ;* gora, *to clip, to diminish ;* goraz, *to hew down ;* gorar, *to saw ;* garzen, *a small axe, a hatchet :* Gearr, *cut.*

Gab, *a back, convex surface, eminence ;* givoul, *risen in body, ripe :* Cab, *a head.*

Gevoul, *a border of territory;* ooval, *to border, to partition* (the idea is something raised); from Hebrew oab; also like Gaelic Balla, *a wall; ge* prefixed.

Govoh, *a hill;* oovoh, *to heighten;* oovah, *high;* gaavoh, *pride;* oevouha, *high;* gibbain, *a humpback:* Cab, *a head*

Gibbour, *a mighty one, a giant:* Cab, *a head; our* like fear (in composition—ear), *a man.*

Goulee, *a captire;* oolooth, *captivity:* oolon, *to drive captive:* Gille, *a lad, a servant, a gilly* (the *g* hard), *a ghilly.*

Geer, *chalk;* oeero (Syriac), *plaster:* Cre, *earth.*

Geesh, *a clod;* perhaps like Ce, *earth.*

Gav, *vaulted, arched:* Cam, *bent.*

Gouv, *a den;* like Hebrew oav; also like Gaelic Uamh, *a cave; g* prefixed.

Geve, *a cistern;* like Hebrew gav; also like Gaelic Gabh, *take, receive.*

Gouveem, *diggers, husbandmen:* Ce, *the ground.*

Gorar, *to stir up, to proroke:* Geur, *sharp.*

Gorad, *to scratch:* Gearr, *cut;* geur, *sharp;* garbh, *rough.*

Gorov, *scurvy:* perhaps like Garbh, *rough.*

Goroun, *the throat:* perhaps like Garbh, *rough, hard.*

Geled, *a covering:* Cleidh, *hide, conceal.*

Gomol, *a camel:* Camal, *a camel;* cam, *crooked;* al (obs.), *a horse.* The fitting-in of two Gaelic words to form camal is perhaps accidental.

Golal, *to roll;* oilgol, *the globe, a wheel;* gullah, *a bowl;* golam, *to fold up;* ogeel, *a ring;* oulgouleth, *a skull;* oulloh, *a cup;* oilyouneem, *a head-dress;* agoleem, *round drops;* golam, *a large loose garment round the person;* gol, *a heap of stones:* with all these there is connected the idea of roundness, like Gaelic Calbh, *a head.*

Godah, *to cut down;* in meaning a little like Gath, *a sting, a dart, &c.,* the idea being something penetrating.

Gedoud, *a troop:* Cath, *a company of soldiers.*

Gomo, *to sup up:* Gabh, *take, receive.*

Gaviah, *a cup:* Cub, *bend* (the idea being something hollow).

SECOND GROUP.

An initial *g* is either added in Hebrew or omitted in Gaelic; either *g* or *g* followed by a vowel-sound: about fourteen instances.

Gohar, g-ohar, *to breathe:* Athar, *air.*

Gova, g-ova, *to waste away, to dissolve:* Abh, *water.*

Gephen, ge-phen, *a vine:* Fion, *wine.*

GOLAKH, go-lakh, *to shave* (the idea is to make smooth): Leac, *a flat stone* (hence cromlech).

GEVOOROH, ge-vooroh, *great strength;* GEVER, go-ver, *a man of strength;* GEVERETH, ge-vereth, *a female in power:* Mor, *great;* or barr, *top.*

GORAPH, go-raph, *to carry off, to seize:* Reub, *tear.*

GOZAR, go-zar, *to cut;* GEZAIROH, *cut off, separated:* Soarr, *cut.*

GODAL, go-dal, *to elevate;* GODOUL, *great, tall;* GOUDEL, gou-del, *greatness:* Tula, *a hill.*

GOUV, g-ouv (Chaldee), *a den:* Uamh, *a cave.*

THIRD GROUP.

An initial *s* is either omitted in Hebrew or added in Gaelic.

GOLOH, *to discover, to reveal:* like Glaodh, *call;* but also like Sgeul, *a tale.* Under the letter kaph, see Hebrew KONOPH, kon-oph, like Gaelic Sgiathan. Under the letter koph, see Hebrew KOOT, like Gaelic Sgeith; Hebrew KEE, like Gaelic Sgeith; Hebrew KAIN, like Gaelic Sgian: instances where *s* is similarly treated.

DALETH.

The fourth Hebrew letter. It was so named from being in shape like the opening into a tent (akin to Gaelic Toll, *a hole*). From deleth comes delta, the name of the fourth Greek letter: the shape of this is exactly that of the opening into a tent)

Some Hebrew and Gaelic words are alike in meaning and sound, except that an initial *d* is either added in Hebrew or omitted in Gaelic; either *d* or *d* followed by a vowel-sound.

FIRST GROUP.

Words which begin with *d* in Hebrew, and with *d* or *t* in Gaelic.

DALETH, *the name of the fourth Hebrew letter;* DELETH, *the opening into a tent;* and then applied to the door itself; a lid: Toll, *a hole.*

DOOM, *to be silent, to be dumb;* DOMAM, *to be silent;* DOMON, *to silence;* DOMEE, *quietness:* Tamh, *rest, quietness.* From the Celtic Tamh, the rivers Tay, Thames, Tamar, Tavy, and other streams take their name, the idea being a smoothly-flowing river.

DOMON, *to silence;* metaphorically *to cut off, to slay.* It may be the same word as the above, but also like Teum, *cut, cut off.*

DEYOU, *ink:* Dubh, *ink.*

DOVAK, *to cleave to:* perhaps like Do, *to* (the preposition turned into a verb).

DEREKH, *a way:* Direach, *straight;* or rach, *go; d* prefixed.

DESHEN, *ashes;* DOSHAN, *to cleanse from ashes:* Teas, *heat.*

DOTH, *an edict;* DOTH (Chaldee), *law:* Dith, *condemn.*

DOL, *exhausted, poor;* DALLOH, *exhaustion:* Duile, *a mournful, helpless creature.*

DOLAKH, *to disturb, to trouble:* Diulich, *difficult.*

DOYAIK, *a wooden turret or shed used in besieging towns, and under which the besiegers were able to approach the walls:* Tigh, teach, *a house.*

SECOND GROUP.

An initial *d* is either added in Hebrew or omitted in Gaelic; either *d,* or *d* followed by a vowel-sound.

DAD, *a nipple, a teat:* At, *a swelling, a prominence.*

DIBBAIR, d-ibbair, *to speak;* DOVOR, *a word:* Abair, *say.*

DOMOH, *to compare;* DEMOOTH, *likeness:* Amhuil, amh-uil, *like.*

DOAG, *to be troubled, anxious;* DOKHAL (Syriac), *to fear;* DAAGOH, *anxiety:* Eagal, *fear.*

DOUVER, dou-ver, *a pasture:* Feur, *grass.*

DOGAR, do-gar, *to cherish:* Gradh, *lore.*

DOKAR, do-kar, *to thrust through:* Gearr, *cut.*

DORAKH, do-rakh, *to tread:* Rach, *go.*

DEROUR, de-rour, *flowing:* Ruith, *flow.*

THIRDLY.

DOLAPH, dol-aph, *to drop* like water, like Latin stillo, which like Sil, *drop.*

HE.

The fifth Hebrew letter.

Some Hebrew and Gaelic words are alike in meaning and sound, except that an initial *h* is either added in Hebrew or omitted in Gaelic; either *h,* or *h* followed by a vowel-sound.

FIRST GROUP.

An initial *h* is either added in Hebrew or omitted in Gaelic.

HOO, *he:* E, *he.*

HEE, *she:* I, *she.*

HAI, *the:* A, *the.*

HOH, *an exclamation:* Eigh, *a shout, a cry.*

HOUEE, *alas;* HOEE, *alas;* HOH, *alas;* HEE, *woe:* Och, *alas.* Gaelic is partial to the sound *ch,* as is seen in tulach, *a hill,* from tula, *a hill.*

HILLAIL, *to praise:* Alladh, *praise, renown.*

HOULAIL, *mad, raging:* Alluidh, *wild.*

HEELOH, *to bring up:* Al, *nourish.*

HORAG, *to kill:* Ar, *kill.*

HOGOH, *to utter;* HEGEH, *utterance:* Eigh, *a shout,* or guth, *a voice.*

HOHAIM, *the same, like:* Amhuil, amh-uil, *like.*

HORAS, *to throw down;* perhaps like Uir, *the ground.*

HAIREEM, *raise up:* Ard, *high;* or beir, *support; b* omitted.

HORIZOUTH, *a pregnant woman;* HOROH, *to conceive;* perhaps Ard; or beir, *to take hold.*

HOR, *a mount, a mountain;* like Ard, *high;* ord, *a hill.*

HAISHEEV, *to bring back:* Ais, *back, backwards;* aisig, *return.*

HOOSEEPH, *to add to, to increase:* Ais (obs.), *a hill.*

HAIAIZ, *to strengthen:* Ais (obs.), *a stronghold.*

SECOND GROUP.

An initial *he* is either added in Hebrew or omitted in Gaelic.

HOPHAIR, ho-phair, *to destroy:* Bruth, *bruise;* or brath, *fire.*

HOCAR, ho-car, *to be perverse:* Car, *a turn.*

HOKHAIN, ho-khain, *established:* Comhnuidh, *a dwelling.*

HIKHOTH, hi-khoth, *to strike, to smite:* Gath, *a dart.*

HOVEEN, ho-veen, *to cause to understand:* Mein, *mind.*

HAIKOL, hai-kol, *a temple; kol* perhaps akin to Cladh, *a mound, a dyke a trench;* also perhaps akin to clachan, *a village.*

HASKAIL, ha-skail, *prudence;* HISKEEL hi-skeel, *to be prudent:* Ciall, *sense; s* prefixed; *ha* prefixed.

THIRD GROUP.

An initial consonant is either omitted in Hebrew or added in Gaelic; this is a conjecture offered for the consideration of the reader. See the third group under the letter aleph, the third group under the letter ayin, and the second group under the letter yod.

HOYOH, *to be:* perhaps Bi, bith, *to be; b* omitted.

HOLAM, *to strike:* Buail, *strike; b* omitted.

HOLAM, *to place at a distance:* Buail, *throw; b* omitted.

HORAS, *to break down:* Bris, *break; b* omitted.

HOMOH, *to make a noise:* Fuaim, *noise; f* omitted.

HOUNOH, *to defraud:* Faoin, *vain, empty; f* omitted.

HOLAKH, h-ol-akh, *to walk:* Falbh, *go; f* omitted.

HOVOH, *to give:* Gabh, *take; g* omitted.

HODAD, *to shout; hod* like Guth, *a voice; g* omitted.

HARESAH, *a ruinous place:* Garbh, *rough, rugged; g* omitted.

VOV or VAU.

The sixth Hebrew letter.

V as a vowel, as U, *again;* like Gaelic Ath, *again.* The Gaelic ath, *again,* perhaps akin to Gaelic da, *two.*

ZAIN.

The seventh Hebrew letter.

Some Hebrew and Gaelic words are alike in meaning and sound, except that either the Hebrew prefixes z, or the Gaelic omits this sound at the beginning of a word; either *z,* or *z* followed by a vowel-sound.

FIRST GROUP.

Hebrew words beginning with *z,* and Gaelic words beginning with *s.*

ZONOV, *a tail:* perhaps like Sin, *extend.*

ZEROUA, *an arm;* ZOROU, *to scatter, spread abroad:* Sreath, *a row, a line.*

ZEH, *this:* So, *this.*

ZOR, *strange, excluded:* perhaps like As, *out, out of.*

SECOND GROUP.

Either initial *z* is added in Hebrew, or a similar sound is omitted in Gaelic; either *z,* or *z* followed by a vowel-sound.

ZOKAR, *to remember:* Cridhe (pronounced cri), *the heart:* the heart figuratively supposed to be the seat of the mind.

ZOAK, *to cry out:* Eigh, *a shout.*

ZORAM, *to overflow:* Ruith, *flow.*

ZOV, *flowing, running:* Abh, *water.*

ZOOD, *to seethe:* Ad (obs.), *water.*

ZOOH, *sweat:* O (obs.), *water; z* prefixed.

ZOKAPH, *to raise up:* Gabh, *take.*

ZORAKH, *to rise as the sun:* Eirich, *rise.*

ZAAPH, *violent rage;* ZOAPH, *to enrage; za* prefixed. perhaps like Fuath, *rage.*

ZEEKOUTH, *sparks:* Gath, *a ray of light.*

ZOMAR, *to chant; z* prefixed: *omar* like Abair, *say* (the Gaelic can signifies *to say, to sing;* hence Latin cano).

ZOKAIN, zo-kain, *an old man:* perhaps like Can (obs.), *white;* or like sean, *old;* a *k* or *c* lost in Celtic.

ZOKH, *clear;* ZOKHOH, *to make clean, to wash;* ZOKHOO, *purity;* ZOKAK,
to cleanse; ZEEKHOOKETH, *crystal, glass;* ZOAKH, *to extinguish,*
suppose to pour water over; z prefixed : *okh* like *aig* in Gaelic
Aigeann, *the sea,* and aigeal, *a pool* (hence Latin aqua).

KHETH.

The eighth Hebrew letter. In sound like the Greek chi, or like *ch*
in loch as the Scotch pronounce it. Like *ch* hard. Here represented
by *kh.*

Some Hebrew and Gaelic words are alike in meaning and sound,
except that either the Hebrew prefixes *kh,* or the Gaelic omits *c* or *g*
at the beginning of a word. Hebrew is partial to this sound at the
beginning of a word, and Gaelic at the end of a word.

FIRST GROUP.

Hebrew words beginning with *kh,* and Gaelic words beginning with
c or *g.*

KHONOH, *to encamp;* KHANUYOUTH, *places of rest.* Under the letter
kaph, see KOON, *to erect;* KAN, *a basis, a pedestal;* KONAS, KONASH,
to gather into a place of security: under the letter koph, see KAN,
a nest; KONAN, *to make a nest:* under the letter shin, see SHEKHAN,
a resting-place: also see MAKHANEH, *a camp;* GAN, *a garden;*
GONAN, *to enclose;* MEKHOUNOH, *a foundation, a base;* NOKHOUN,
certain, fixed; HOKHAIN, *established;* OKHAIN, *surely so.*
Of KHONOH, KONAS, GONAN, and KONAN, the idea is an enclosure.
All these Hebrew words are akin to each other, and to the Gaelic
Comhnuidh, comhn-uidh, *a dwelling:* An comhnuidh, *habitually.*

KHORAD, *to tremble :* Crith, *shake.*

KHORAG, *to force, to drive out* part of it, like KHORAM, *to devote* for good
or evil : Cuir, *set, place.*

KHORATS, *move quickly :* Grad, *move quickly.*

KHOOG, *a circle;* KHAKOH, *a fish-hook;* KHOKH, *a ring to put in an
animal's nose;* KHOGAG, *to move in a circle;* KHAGOUROH, *a girdle,
a belt;* KHAIK, *the bosom;* KHOGAR, *to gird about;* KHAIKH, *the
palate;* KHOKAK, *to impress, to engrave* (the idea is something
hollowed as a cup is): of all these the idea is roundness, or
hollowness, or both: like Gaelic Cuach, *a cup; the basin in the
hollow of a hill; a curl.*

KHARTSOOV, *torment :* Cruaidh, *painful.*

KHOROH, *fierce;* KHOROH, *to be kindled* (applied to anger); Geur,
fierce.

KHOMAK, *to linger;* KHOUMER, *clay; potter's clay; mortar for building;* KHOUMER, a homer, *a measure of capacity;* KHOOMOZ, *a buckle:* Cum, *hold, withhold.*

KHOLOOTS, *drawn back, rescued:* Cul, *behind.*

KHAIT, *a sin;* a little like Ciont, *a sin.*

KHOVAT, *to beat off:* Caob, *strike.*

KHILLOH, *to supplicate:* Cli, *humble.*

KHORAPH, *to reproach, to slander:* perhaps like Gaoir, *noise.*

KHOMAD, *to desire eagerly, to covet:* Caomh, *dear.*

KHOOL, *to be sorrowful:* Gul, *lament.*

KHORAD, *care:* perhaps like Curam, *care.*

KHORASH, *to grave; to plough; to cut out; to fabricate;* KHOURAISH, *an artificer,* as in wood; KHERET, *a graving-tool, an iron pen;* KHOROOTS, *sharp;* KHOROOTH, *to engrave;* KHOROOL, *a thorn-bush;* KHEREV, *a sword, a weapon;* KHERMAIS, kher-mais, *a sickle, a scythe:* Gearr, *cut;* geur, *sharp.*

KHALLOH, *a cake,* if round, perhaps from its shape; KHALAKHOTH, *a caldron,* from its round shape: Calbh, *a head.*

KHAITS, *an arrow;* KHEEDOH, *sharp;* KHIDOUTH, *sharp sayings, riddles;* KHADDOH, *sharp;* KHOOTS, *a thorn;* KHEDEK, khed-ek, *a brier;* KHOTAV, *to cut wood;* KHOTOH, *to cast out;* KHOTSAV, *to hew out of a rock;* KHOTSOH, *to divide;* KHOUTER, *a twig, a shoot, a rod:* of all these the idea is sharp, penetrating, cutting: like Gaelic Gath, *a sting, a dart, a javelin, an arrow.*

KHONAN, *to implore:* Caoin, *to lament.*

KHAIN, *favour;* KHONAN, *to be gracious:* Caoin, *pleasant.*

KHOUR, *a hole:* Cro, *anything round.*

KHOOR, *white, pale;* KHOUROB, *white linen;* KHORI, *a nobleman dressed in white:* Ciar, *grey.*

KHONAG, *to strangle, to choke:* Cuing, *a yoke.*

KHOPHO, *to cover over;* KHUPOH, *a canopy, cover, protection:* Cab, *a head.*

KHALEE, *a jewel for the neck:* perhaps akin to Caol, *small, narrow* (might be applied to the neck: from caol comes Latin columna).

KHANEETH, *a javelin:* Guin, *wound, pierce.*

KHOVO, *to hide:* Cub, *bend the body, crouch.*

KHOLOV, *milk;* khol like Geal, *white.*

KHOPHATS, *to desire;* KHAIPHETS, *delight:* Gabh, *take; conceive; kindle.*

KHAIL, *a fortification, a bulwark;* KHELKOH, *a portion of ground;* KHAILEK, *a portion, an inheritance:* Cladh, *a trench, a dyke, a stone-wall, a mound.*

c

KHODAL, *to cease, to forbear :* perhaps akin to Codal, *sleep.*

KHALOMEESH, *flint :* Clach, *a stone.*

KHOLAL, *to wound, to kill :* perhaps akin to Gaelic Clach, *a stone,* as stones were used in attack (both by themselves and in slings), and stoning was a form of judicial execution. Also like lia, *a stone ; kh* prefixed.

KHAIREEM, *enclosed in a net :* Car, *a turn.*

KHOUVER, *a waste place :* Garbh, *rough, rugged.*

KHOVAIR, *a companion :* Comh, *together ;* fear, *a man.*

KHOVERETH, *a joining :* Comh, *together ;* beir, *bear.*

KHOSHAV, *to think, to reckon :* Cuis, *a matter ; a cause ; a reason.*

KHALEETSOUTH, *change of dresses :* perhaps like Cleidh, *hide, conceal.*

KHOTATH, *to make anxious :* Guidh, *beseech.*

KHOLEEL, *a tube, a hollow instrument ;* KHOLEL, *a player on a wind-instrument :* Cuilc, *a cane, a reed.*

KHALATZ, *the loin ;* KHALOTSEEN, *loins :* perhaps like Cul, *the back.*

KHALOUN, khal-oun, *a window* (see KHAVVEEN): perhaps akin to Geal, *white.*

KHOULAIK, *a partner* (see KALOH, *a spouse*): Coile, *a spouse ; a husband ;* ceile akin to gaol, *love.*

SECOND GROUP.

Either the Hebrew prefixes *kh,* or the Gaelic omits initial *c* or *g.*

KHEVEL, *a rope, a cord ;* KHOUVAIL, *a cable ;* KHOVEL, *a ship-man, a sailor ;* from using ropes much : Ball, *a cable.*

KHAVVEEN, kha-vveen (Syriac), *a window :* perhaps akin to Ban, *white* (see KHALOUN).

KHOPHAR, kho-phar, *to blush :* Brath, *fire.*

KHAVOLEEM, *spoilers ;* vol like Buail, *smite.*

KHABOOROH, *a boil ; boor* like Barr, *a swelling ;* or brath, *fire.*

KHABUROUTH, *swellings, blows ;* like Barr, *a height, a swelling ;* or caob, *strike.*

KHOROH, *to contend :* Ar, *fight.*

KHOLOK, *smooth :* Leac, *a flat stone* (cromlech is partly from this).

KHAMMAN, *an image :* Amhuil, amh-uil, *like.*

KHITTO, *to cleanse* (suppose to wash): Ad (obs.), *water.*

KHUK, KHOUK, *a decree, a statute* (suppose a proclamation): Eigh, *a shout.*

KHODOH, *to rejoice :* Ait, *joyful.*

KHASEEN, KHOUSEN, *strength ;* KHOUSEN, KHOZAK, *strong ;* KHOZAK, *to strengthen ;* Ais (obs.), *a stronghold.*

KHOZEK, *a breast;* KHOUSHEN, *a breast-plate:* Ais (obs.), *a hill.*

KHOVAL, *to twist:* Fill, *fold.*

KHOUMOH, *a circumvallation wall:* Uim, *around.*

KHAYIL, *an army.* Under the letter kaph, see KOL, *all;* KOLOH, *to complete;* KOHOL, *an assembly;* KOHAL, *to assemble;* KOUL, *all things, everything:* under the letter koph, see KOHOL, *an assembly;* KOHAL, *to assemble:* all these Hebrew words are akin to each other, and to the Gaelic Uile, *all.*

AKHAR, *after;* AKHOURAI, *the hinder parts;* AKHOURANEETH, *back again;* AKHAREETH, *latter, last;* AKHAIR, *another,* from AKHAR, *after* (these are given also under the letter aleph): Iar, *after; kh* prefixed; and then *a* prefixed.

KHOUSHEKH, khou-shekh, *dark;* KHASHAIKOH, *darkness:* Sgiath, *a shade.*

TETH.

Some Hebrew and Gaelic words are alike in meaning and sound, except that an initial *t* is either added in Hebrew, or omitted in Gaelic; either *t,* or *t* followed by a vowel-sound.

Hebrew words beginning with *t,* and Gaelic words beginning with *d* or *t.*

TEEROH, *a castle, a tower:* Tur, *a tower;* torr, *a hill.*

TOOR (Chaldee and Syriac), *a mount:* Torr, *a hill.*

TOAN, *to load:* perhaps like Dun, *a hill* (a heap).

TOMAM, *to cover over:* Tom, *a hill* (a heap).

TOOH, *to err:* Taobh, *a side.*

TOKHAN, *to grind, to make small:* a little like Tana, *thin.*

TOAM, *to taste, to eat a little:* Teum, *bite.*

TORAKH, *to weary:* Teirig, *waste.*

TOHAR, *to cleanse* (suppose to wash); TOHOOR, *clean:* Doir, *water.*

TEEROH, *a castle, a tower:* Tur, *a tower;* torr, *a hill.*

TOUAR, *of a fine form;* akin to TEEROH.

SECOND GROUP.

An initial *t* is either added in Hebrew, or omitted in Gaelic; either *t,* or *t* followed by a vowel-sound.

TAAM, *manner;* the *m* like Modh, *manner.*

TOVA, t-ova, *to sink;* TOVAL, t-oval, *to dip:* Abh (obs.), *water.*

TOUV, tou-v, *good;* the *v* like Ba (obs.), *good; b* changed to *v.* See under Hebrew YOTAV, *to make good.*

TEREM, te-rem, *before :* Roi, *before.*

Toov, *a row :* perhaps like Sreath, *a row ; s* omitted ; *t* prefixed. See under the letter tov, TOUV, *a row.*

YOD.

The tenth Hebrew letter.

Some Hebrew and Gaelic words are alike in meaning and sound, except that either the Hebrew prefixes *y*, or the Gaelic omits this sound at the beginning of a word.

FIRST GROUP.

An initial *y* either added in Hebrew, or this sound omitted in Gaelic ; either *y*, or *y* followed by a vowel-sound : about twenty-nine instances.

YABELETH, *a wen, a swelling; bel* like Ball, *a round object.*

YAISH, *existence :* Is, *am.*

YOTSO, *to go out :* Uidhe, *a step.*

YODA, *to know :* Aithnich, aith-nich, *know.*

YORO, *to saturate ;* YEOUR, *a river :* Ruith, *flow.*

YODD, *to appoint, to assemble ;* YATSEEV (Syriac), *fixed :* Aite, *a place.*

YELEL, *a babe ;* YELED, *a child ;* YOLAD, *to beget ;* YELDOH, *a girl :* Al, *young ; young of any kind ; a brood ; a generation :* alaich, *bring forth.*

YOSAR, *to chastise :* perhaps like Ais, *behind.*

YOUM, *a day :* Am, *time.*

YITHMARMOR, yith-mar-mor, *to embitter ; yith* prefixed ; *mar* like Muir, *the sea ; mar* repeated.

YESOUD, *foundation ;* YOSAD, *to found ;* YOSHAV, *to sit :* Suidh, *sit, place.*

YORASH, *to inherit, to succeed :* perhaps like Iar, *after.*

YOHEER, *superb :* Ard, *high.*

YOSHPAIH, *a jasper ; precious stones of different colours ; yosh* like Hebrew AISH, *fire,* like Gaelic Teas, *heat.*

YERAKH, *a month :* Re, *the moon.*

YOM, *the sea ;* YAIMEEM, *springs of water :* Abh, *water ; bh* to *m.*

YOSHON, *old ;* YOSHAN, *to grow old :* Sean, *old.*

YOSHAN, yo-shan, *to sleep :* Suain, *sleep.*

YORAT, *to hinder, to keep back :* perhaps like Iar, *behind.*

YOSHOR, *straight, just :* Sreath, *a row, a line.*

YOGOH, *to grieve ;* Och, *alas.*

YOGA, *to exert, to work :* Achd, *do.*

YOVASH, *to dry up, to wither :* Fas, *lay waste.*

YOGAR, *to fear :* Crith, *tremble.*

YOTAV, *to amend, to improve, make good ;* yo prefixed ; *t* prefixed ; the
v like Ba (obs.), *good.* See under Hebrew TOUV, *good.*

In all the above an initial *y* is either added in Hebrew, or omitted
in Gaelic.

SECOND GROUP.

A conjectural affinity is offered for the consideration of the reader :
perhaps an initial consonant either omitted in Hebrew, or added
in Gaelic. The instances where *f* is either omitted or added
are very clear, and if one consonant be so treated, why not another ? See the third group under the letter aleph ; the third group
under the letter he ; and the third group under the letter ayin.

YORO, *to fear :* Crith, *tremble ; c* omitted.

YODOH, *to throw :* Gath, *a dart ; g* omitted.

YOHAV, *give :* Gabh, *take ; g* omitted.

YOUREH, *rain :* Doir, *water ; d* omitted.

YEKEV, *a wine-vault, a cellar ;* ye prefixed; *k* prefixed; *ev* like Gaelic
Uamh, *a cave.*

In the next ten words, an initial *f* either omitted in Hebrew, or
added in Gaelic.

YAYIN, *wine :* Fion, *wine.*

YEREK, *green ;* YEROKOUN, *green, greenish ;* YARIOKOUN, *pale green :*
Feur, *grass.*

YAAR, *a forest :* Fridh, *a forest.*

YOSAPH, *to increase :* Fas, *to grow.*

YONON, *to defraud :* Faoin, *foolish, idle.*

YAANEH, *with great noise :* Fonn, *an air, a tune, a sound.*

YIDOUNEE, *a prognostication ;* yid like Faidh, *a prophet.*

YOLAKH, y-ol-ak, *to walk* (see HOLAKH) : Falbh, *go.*

KAPH.

The eleventh Hebrew letter—kaph or coph. Sometimes represented
by *c ;* sometimes by *k ;* it is here represented by *k.*

Some Hebrew and Gaelic words are alike in meaning and sound,
except that either the Hebrew prefixes *k,* or the Gaelic omits this sound
at the beginning of a word ; either *k,* or *k* followed by a vowel-sound.

FIRST GROUP.

Words which begin with *k* in Hebrew, and with *c* or *g* in Gaelic.

KOUHAIN, *a priest :* perhaps from the Hebrew word *to perform duty.*
Also like Gaelic Can (obs.), *white* (he wore white vestments).

Kouhain, *a priest;* kehounoh, *the priestly office;* from koon, *to fix;* from his performing fixed duties. See under koon, *to fix;* akin to Comhnuidh, *a dwelling, a fixed abode.*

Koon, *to fix, erect;* kan, *a basis, a pedestal;* konas, konash (Chaldee), *to gather into a place of security.* Under the letter koph, see kan, *a nest;* konan, *to make a nest:* under the letter kheth, see khonoh, *to encamp:* also see makhaneh, *a camp;* gan, *a garden;* gonan, *to enclose.* Of all these, the idea is an enclosure. Also see tekhoonoh, *establishment, estate, property;* tikhoun, *established;* mekhounoh, *a foundation, a base;* shekhan, *a resting-place.* All these Hebrew words are akin to each other, and to the Gaelic Comhnuidh, comhn-uidh, *a dwelling.*

Kinnoh, *to name:* Cinneach, *a surname.*

Kool, *to hold up:* Gabhail, *take.*

Kelouv, *a basket:* Cliabh, *a basket.*

Kephour, *a large cup:* Gabh, *take, receive.*

Kikhaish, *to deceive:* Caog, *wink, connive.*

Koloh, *dim;* Ceil, *hide, shelter.*

Korhan, *to decline:* Cub, *bend.*

Korhath (Syriac), *to fetter:* perhaps like Cub, *bend.*

Kora, *to kneel, to bend:* Car, *a turn, a twist.*

Keroov, *a cherub;* ker perhaps like Gradh, *favour, love.*

Kool, *to comprehend:* Ciall, *sense, reason.*

Korath, *to make agreement;* koraz (Syriac), *an edict:* Gaoir, *noise* (suppose a proclamation).

Kouhain, *a chief person:* Ceann, *a head.*

Kolo, *to confine, constrain:* Cul, *back;* culaig, *an impediment.*

Kidoun, *a lance, a spear:* Gath, *a dart, a javelin.*

Keedoudeem, *sparks of fire:* Gath, *a ray of light.*

Kona, *to humble:* Caoin, *to lament.*

Kouva, *a helmet;* kovood, *stately:* Cab, *a head.*

Kour, *a certain measure:* perhaps like Cro, *anything round.*

Koshal, *to stumble:* perhaps like Cos, *a foot.*

Kaph, *the palm of the hand; the sole of the foot* (the idea is something hollow): Cub, *bend.*

Koroh, *to prepare a banquet:* Cuirm, *a feast.*

Kelev, *a dog;* ke like Cu, *a dog.*

Korath, *to cut;* kouraith, *a feller, a cutter;* karkar, *to root out;* koro (Chaldee), *to pierce;* koras, *to devour;* karkar, *to root out* (*kar* repeated): Gearr, *cut;* geur, *sharp.*

KALOH, *a bride;* KELOOLOH, *bridal state* (see KHOULAIK, *a partner*):
Ceile, *a spouse;* ceile is akin to gaol, *love.*

KORAH, *a beam of wood;* a little like Crann, *a beam.*

KETHOUVETH, *a writing;* see Hebrew AIT, *an iron pen:* perhaps like
Gath, *a dart,* &c. (the idea being something pointed).

KEEYOUR, *a basin;* KIKOR, *a loaf* (from its shape?): Cro, *anything
round.*

KAVOH, *to extinguish:* Cab, *a head* (the idea is putting something
over it).

KERYAH, *a place for cattle:* Cro, *an enclosure; a sheep-cote; a wattled
fold.*

KEPHEL, *a couple, two:* Cupall, *a couple, a pair* (perhaps cupall is not
good Gaelic).

KEED (Arabic), *a misfortune:* perhaps like Gath, *a sting.*

KILYAH, *a kidney:* perhaps akin to Cul, *back* (placed at the back).

SECOND GROUP.

An initial *k* is either added in Hebrew, or omitted in Gaelic; either
k, or *k* followed by a vowel-sound.

KOL, *all;* KOLOH, *to complete;* KOHAL, *to assemble;* KOHOL, *an assembly;*
KOUL, *all things, everything.* Under the letter kheth, see KHAYIL,
an army; under the letter koph, KOHAL, *to assemble;* KOHOL, *an
assembly.* All these Hebrew words are akin to each other, and to
the Gaelic Uile, *all.*

KISSAI, *a chair, a throne:* Suidh, *sit.*

KAR, *a man in power:* Ard, *high.*

KETHER, *a crown;* with *ther* is the idea of roundness, as in Gaelic
Tur, *a tower.*

KABBEER, *valiant; beer* like KOVAR, *to make great:* Mor, *great, mighty;*
m to *b.*

KEPHUAR, *hoar-frost:* Fuar, *cold.*

KOMAR, *to shrivel from heat; mar* like Brath, *fire.*

KALKAIL, *a sustainer, a nourisher:* Al, *to nourish.*

KIPPAIR, *to purify:* Brath, *fire.*

KIKOR, ki-kor, *a level tract of country, surrounded with hills; ki* prefixed;
kor like Gaelic Cars, *a level fertile tract of country,* as the Carse of
Gowrie, Carse of Stirling, &c. The idea is a tract through which
a river runs, and somewhat level as compared with the adjacent
hills: this is a very interesting word. See MEESHOUR, me-shour,
like the Gaelic srath, *a strath.*

THIRD GROUP.

An initial *s* is either omitted in Hebrew, or added in Gaelic.

KONOPH, *a wing:* Sgiathan, *a little wing; s* omitted. Under the letter koph, see Hebrew KOOT like Gaelic sgeith: Hebrew KEE like Gaelic sgeith; Hebrew KAIN like Gaelic sgian: also see Hebrew GOLOH like Gaelic sgeul: instances where *s* is similarly treated.

KEE, *but:* Ach, *but; a* omitted.

LAMED.

The twelfth Hebrew letter.

Some Hebrew and Gaelic words are alike in meaning and sound, except that an initial *l* is either added in Hebrew, or omitted in Gaelic; either *l,* or *l* followed by a vowel-sound.

Some Hebrew words beginning with *l* are in meaning and sound like Gaelic words, except that the Gaelic words begin with *c* or *g;* an initial *c* or *g* either omitted in Hebrew, or added in Gaelic.

FIRST GROUP.

Words which begin with *l* in both languages.

LOAKH, *a tablet of stone* (*also a tablet of wood or metal*); LEKHEE, *a cheek* (perhaps the idea is a flat surface); LEKHEM, *bread* (perhaps from its shape; flat cakes?); Leac, *a flat stone* (as in cromlech).

LESHEM, *an agate,* a whitish stone: perhaps like Lia, *grey.*

LOVAT, *to stumble:* Lub, *crouch, bend.*

LOPHATH, *to shrink, to contract:* Lub, *bend.*

SECOND GROUP.

An initial *l* is either added in Hebrew, or omitted in Gaelic; either *l,* or *l* followed by a vowel-sound.

LEMAALOH, *high:* Meall, *a hill.*

LESHORAITH, *to minister to, to serve:* Saothair, *work, labour.*

LOVAN, *to whiten;* LIVNOH, *whiteness;* LIVNOH, *a poplar* (a whitish tree); LEVONOH, *the moon;* all these like Gaelic Ban, *white.*

LEVONOH, *the moon;* LUAN, *the moon.* The Hebrew for *moon* is akin to the Hebrew for *white.* In LIVNOH, *li* prefixed; *vn* like Gaelic Ban, *white.* In Gaelic, gealach is the *moon,* and geal is *white.*

LEVAINOH, *a brick,* like Hebrew EVEN, *a stone;* which see: Hebrew EVEN akin to Gaelic Ban, *white.*

LEOOMATH, *agreeable, corresponding to:* Amhuil, amh-uil, *like.*

LA, *no, not, none, nothing:* perhaps like Cha (pronounced ha), *not; l* prefixed.

At the beginning of a word, *c* or *g* is either omitted in Hebrew, or added in Gaelic.

LAHAV, *a blade, the glittering part of a sword; a flame; flaming;* LAPEED, *a flame;* LAPPEED, *a torch, a flame;* in LAP-EED, *lap* like LAHAV, the *v* changed to *p*: Claidheamh, *a sword* (the French glaive and Scotch claymore).

LOVOH, *to join:* Cuile, *a spouse; a husband.*

LOAT, *to conceal;* LOOT, *to wrap up:* Cleidh, *hide, conceal.*

LEVOOSH, *garments, clothing;* le like Cleidh, *hide, cover.*

LOKAKH, *to take;* LOKAD, *to take by force, to conquer;* LOKAT, *to collect, to pick up;* LOKASH, *to glean;* LOKAK, *to lap, to lick* (that is, to take); LOKHAKH, *to clear away, to eat up entirely;* LOKHATS, *to oppress:* all these like Gaelic Glac, *to take; g* omitted.

LOTHATH, *to cry out:* Glaodh, *to call.*

LOVA, *the gullet, the throat:* Caol, *narrow.*

LAOIZ, *a strange language:* Gall, *a lowlander; a foreigner: one ignorant of the Gaelic language.*

MEM.

The thirteenth Hebrew letter. As the wavy appearance of the top of the letter is like the ripples on the surface of water, there is an idea that Mem received its name from Mayim, *waters,* plural of mabuah, *a stream;* this like Gaelic Abh, *water; m* prefixed.

Some Hebrew and Gaelic words are alike in meaning and sound, except that an initial *m* is either added in Hebrew, or omitted in Gaelic; either *m,* or *m* followed by a vowel-sound.

Words which begin with *m* in both languages.

MAALOH, *a height, a cliff;* MAAL, *above;* MAALOH, *a degree, a step:* Meall, *a hill;* maol, *a promontory, a mull* (as in Mull of Cantire, Mull of Galloway).

MELEKH, *a king;* MALKOH, *a queen;* MOLAKH, *to reign:* perhaps akin to Hebrew MAAL, *above,* like Meall, *a hill.*

MOAD, *a place of assembly:* Mod, *an assembly.*

MOOH, *bowels;* MEOUHEE (Syriac), *entrails:* a little like Mionach, *bowels.*

MELOKHOH, *labour, work:* Meil, *grind.*

MOOK, *to mock:* Mag, *to mock* (is mag good Gaelic?)

MEOUD, *exceedingly*: Mo, *more*.

MOROUM, *high, lofty*; like Mor, *great*; or ard, *high* (*m* prefixed).

MOSAKH, *to mingle liquids*: Measg, *to mix*.

MOKHOR, *to-morrow*: Maireach, *to-morrow*.

MINDA (Chaldee), *intelligence*: Moin, *mind*.

MOKHO, *to smite together, to squeeze*: Much, *squeeze*.

MAISEEM, *consideration*: Meas, *esteem*.

MEOUD, *exceedingly*: Mo, *more*.

MORAR, *to embitter*; MARMAR, *to embitter*; *mar* repeated: Muir, *the sea*.

MORATS, *to be vehement*: perhaps like Mor, *great, mighty*; or brath, *fire* (excited).

MOOTH, *to die*: Meath, *fade, decay*.

MITHANNEH, *irritating himself*: Miann, *desire, strong will*.

MAITAV, mai-tav, *best*; *mai* like Mo, *more*. See under tav: in *tav* the *v* like Ba (obs.), *good*; *ta* prefixed.

SECOND GROUP.

Words beginning with *m*, where an initial *m* is either added in Hebrew, or omitted in Gaelic; either *m*, or *m* followed by a vowel-sound.

MIKRO, *reading* (if reading aloud): Gaoir, *a noise*.

MOOUZ, *a strong protection*: Ais (obs.), *a stronghold*.

MOROUM, *height*: Ard, *high*.

MEGOOROH, *a stone-house*; MEKHER, *a fixed place, a habitation*: Cro, *a hut*.

MAAKEH, *a battlement*: Ach, *a bank, a mound*.

MISNEH, *repetition*: Ais, *back, back again*.

MOUTSO, *a pouring*: Ad (obs.), *water*.

MAAKOSH, *to prevent*: perhaps like Au aghaidh, *against*.

MIKHROH, mi-khroh, *a mine*: perhaps akin to Gearr, *cut*; cutting into the ground.

MOGEN, mo-gen, *a potentate, a head*: Ceann, *a head*.

MABUAH, m-abuah, *a stream*: Abh (obs.), *water*.

MOKOUR, *a spring, a fountain*; *kour* perhaps akin to Cro, *anything round* (which a spring is).

MAKHAROSH, *a cutting instrument*; MEGERAH, *a saw, a harrow*: Gearr, *cut*.

MIKRO, *a convocation*: Gaoir, *a noise, a call*.

MAGEED, *a declarer, a reporter*: Guth, *a voice*.

MEKHALELEEM, *piping*; *khal* like Cuile, *a cane, a reed*.

Moog, *to dissolve;* mokak, *to dissolve; oog* like aig, in Aigeal, aig-eal, *a pool;* aigean, *the sea.*

Mokhar, mo-khar, *to sell;* mekheer, me-kheer, *the price:* Creic, *sell;* roic, *sell.*

Makhaneh, *a camp;* mokhoun, *an establishment.* Under the letter khoth, see khonoh, *to encamp:* under the letter kaph, see koon, *to erect;* kan, *a basis;* konas, konash, *to gather into a place of security:* under the letter koph, see kan, *a nest;* konan, *to make a nest:* also see gan, *a garden;* oonan, *to enclose.* Of all these the idea is an enclosure. Also see mekhounoh, *a foundation, a base;* tekhounoh, *establishment, estate, property;* tikhoun, *established.* All these Hebrew words are akin to each other, and to the Gaelic Comhnuidh, comhn-uidh, *a dwelling.*

Moulad, *bringing forth;* mouledeth, *nativity:* Al, *brood; young of any kind;* alaich, *bring forth.*

Moroh, *to rebel:* Ar, *fight.*

Moain, *to refuse; m* prefixed; *n* like Gaelic Neo, *not* (the preposition turned into a verb).

Motor, *slight rain; tor* like Doir, *water.*

Mevakaish, *requesting; vak* like Focal, foc-al, *a word;* also like beue, *utter a sound.*

Mourash, *a possessor:* perhaps like Uir, *land.*

Mahamor, m-aham-or, *a flowing, a torrent; m* prefixed: *am* like Abh, *water; our* like ruith, *flow;* or mor (in composition or), *great.*

Mosas, *to dissolve;* maisheev, *to refresh, revive;* mishka, *sunken, muddy;* maskey, *drink, moisture;* mashkeh, *a moist fertile place;* meshieg, *an overflow; m* prefixed; *os* like Gaelic Uisge, uis-go, *water.* The Hebrew maskey is like whiskey, which is from Gaelic uisge; *m* to *b; b* to *v; v* to *u; u* to *w.*

Maishoreem, *uprightness;* meeshour, *straight:* Sreath, *a line, a row.*

Moshol, *a proverb, a parable:* Sgeul, *a tale.*

Medeenoh, *a province;* akin to Hebrew adounee, *a lord, a governor;* like Gaelic Tanaiste, *a thane.*

Merootsoh, *a race;* mairoots, *a race;* mour, *myrrh* (runs from the tree): Ruith, *run, flow.*

Molai, *full;* millai, *to fill, fulfil, satisfy, complete:* Uile, *all.*

Mareh, *sight, countenance:* Roi, *before; m* prefixed.

Makhabai, ma-khab-ai, *to lurk:* Cub, *crouch.*

Mazreeah, ma-zreeah, *seeding:* Sreath, *a row.*

Mashkeeth, ma-skhoeth, *a destroyer, spoiler:* Sgath, *cut off.*

Meshoraith, me-shoraith, *a minister, attendant:* Saothair, *labour, work.*

MESUKHOH, me-sukhoh, *protection, shelter;* MESOOKHOH, me-sookhoh, *a covering:* Sgiath, *a shade, shelter.*

MISHKOL, mish-kol, *a weight* (see SHOKAL) : Clach, *a stone.*

MAALEH, m-aaleh, *a step, a stair :* Meall, *a hill.*

MOKHATS, mo-khats, *to wound;* MAKHOH, ma-khoh, *a stroke, a blow :* Gath, *a dart, a javelin.*

MENEGED, m-eneged, *in the presence of :* An àghaidh, *against, opposite.*

MAIVEEN, mai-veen, *understanding :* Mein, *mind;* m *to* v.

MASSOUR, ma-ssour, *a saw :* Searr, *cut.*

MEDOOROH, me-dooroh, *a pile, a heap :* Torr, *a hill.*

MEESHOUR, mee-shour, *level ground :* Srath, *a strath, or valley.* Strath occurs in many names of places, as Strathtay, Strathbraan, &c. A strath is the ground on each side of a river ; it is comparatively level as contrasted with the hills which border it. This and Hebrew KIKOR, ki-kor, *a level fertile tract* like the Gaelic Cars, *a carse,* as the Carse of Gowrie, Carse of Stirling, &c., are very interesting words.

MIBAITH, mi-baith, *within, inside, in the house :* Buth, *a booth, pavilion,* Lowland-Scotch *bothy.*

MOUTSO, m-out-so, *a spring :* perhaps like Ad (obs.), *water.*

THIRD GROUP.

The initial letter is m in Hebrew, and b in Gaelic.

M, *from* (prefixed to a substantive); MEM, MIM, *from, out of :* Bho, *from.*

MAILEETS, *an interpreter;* MILLOH, *a word;* MILLAIL, *to converse :* Beul, *the mouth.*

MIZEH, *from this;* m like Bho, *from;* zeh like so, *this.*

MILKHOMOH, *a battle,* perhaps like MALKOUAKH, *booty;* MAHALUMAH, mahal-umah, *a beating:* Buail, *strike.*

MALOKH, *a messenger, angel :* Buail, *throw* (send).

MORAK, *to polish :* Brath, *fire.*

MEREERAI, *bitter destruction;* MORAKH, *to bruise;* MOURAG, *a thrashing instrument :* Bruth, *bruise.*

MOOKH, *to reduce to poverty;* MOOKH, *poor;* MAKHSOUR, *want:* Bochd, *poor.*

MOKH, *a wasting;* MEKHITOH, *dashing to pieces :* Beag, *small.*

MOGAR, *to cast out :* perhaps Bho, *from;* cuir, *to place.*

MAN, *to appoint, constitute;* MENUKHOH, *rest;* MOOUN, *a habitation;* MANNEE (Syriac), *to set, appoint :* Bun, *a foundation.*

MIYOUM, *from the day :* Bho, *from;* am, *time.*

MAIOULOM, *from everlasting;* m like Bho, *from;* aioul like uile, *all;* om like am, *time.*

MEOROII, *a cavern:* Bruth, *a cave.*

MONA, *to avoid, keep back:* perhaps like Bho, *from.*

MEOOROH, *fiery;* MARBEKHETH, *fried:* Brath, *fire.*

MAIREEM, *to raise up:* Beir, *to carry;* or ard, *high;* m prefixed.

MAKAIL, *a walking-stick:* Bachall, *a staff.*

MATTEN, *a staff;* MOUT, *a staff, a pole:* Bat, *a staff.*

MAAYON, *a fountain;* like Hebrew AIN, *a fountain:* Buinne, *a pool in a river* (hence Latin fons).

FOURTH GROUP.

The initial letter is m in Hebrew, and f in Gaelic.

MAANEH, *an answer, a reply:* Fonn, *an air, a tune.*

MALROOSH, *raiment;* MEEEL, *a mantle;* MEULEPHETII, *covered:* Feile, *a covering.*

MESHISSOH, *spoil;* MASHKEETH, *a spoiler;* MOZOH, *to dry up* (if land): Fas, *lay waste.*

MAAZEH, *work:* perhaps like Fas, *grow, increase.*

MOZOUN, *food, nourishment:* Fas, *grow.*

MOAS, *to abhor:* Fuath, *hatred, aversion;* fuathas, *a fright.*

MAREH, *pasture:* Feur, *grass.*

MAHOOL, *a flood;* bool like Fluich, *wet.*

MOTO (Syriac), *stretched out;* MOTHAKH, *to stretch out;* MADAD, *to extend:* Fad, *long.*

MATTO, *a plantation:* Fiodh, *wood.*

FIFTH GROUP.

MAIZAI (Syriac), *to heat;* like Hebrew AISH, *fire;* like Gaelic Teas, *heat.*

MASKEEL, *skilful;* ma prefixed; s prefixed; keel like Ciall, *sense.*

MENSGAIN, *a player, a singer;* gain like Can, *say, sing.*

MAISHEEV, *a restorer,* perhaps like Ais, *back, back again;* sheev like gabh, *take.* See the third group under the letter samech.

MIGROSH, *suburbs;* mi like Uim, *around;* grosh like cathair (the t silent), *a city.*

MAISAV, *a circular seat:* Uim, *around;* suidh, *sit.*

MIGDOL, *a tower;* dol like Tula, *a hill.*

MEDEEVOH, *dissolving, melting;* ed like Ad (obs.), *water;* or eev like abh, *water.*

NUN.

The fourteenth Hebrew letter.

Some Hebrew and Gaelic words are alike in meaning and sound, except that an initial *n* is either added in Hebrew, or omitted in Gaelic; either *n*, or *n* followed by a vowel-sound.

FIRST GROUP.

Words which begin with *n* in both languages.

NEETAM, *obscured ;* like Nochd, *night.*

NEKAIVOH, *a female :* Nighean, *a daughter.*

NIAIR, *to reject :* Neo, *not.*

NOSO, *to lift up :* Nios, *a top, a summit ;* a nios, *up.*

NOZEM, *a nose-ring :* Nios, *a top, a summit.*

 It would be a mistake to suppose that nios was bad Gaelic and a foreign word; the adverb a nios, *up*, is a proof of this.

SECOND GROUP.

An initial *n* is either added in Hebrew, or omitted in Gaelic.

NOSHAKH, *to bite :* Sgath, *cut, bite ; n* prefixed; *s* omitted before *g*.

NOUD, *a leather-bottle :* perhaps like At, *a swelling, a bulging.*

NAID, *a mound :* At, *a swelling, a prominence.*

NOHAK, *to bray :* Eigh, *a cry.*

NOAPH, *to be excited, roused ; noa* prefixed; *ph* like Fuath, *anger.*

NOOPH, *to sprinkle:* Abh, *water.*

NO, *half-boiled :* Amh, *unboiled.*

NOVA, *to flow :* Abh, *water.*

NOVEE, *a prophet ;* NEVOO, *prophecy ;* NIBBO, *to prophesy ; vee* like Faidh, *a prophet.*

NOVVEH, *beautiful ; veh* like Boidheach, *pretty.*

NAKHATH, *rest ; kath* perhaps like Codal, cod-al, *sleep.*

NOVAT, *to investigate, look into :* Beachd, *vision.*

NOUKEPH, *a beating, knocking ;* NOOAPH, *to hurt, to thrust :* Caob, *strike.*

NOVOUN, *full of understanding :* Mein, *mind; m* to *v.*

NOKHOUN, *certain, fixed :* Comhnuidh, *a habitation.* See Hebrew MAKHANEH, *a camp.*

NEKHAIOH, *painful ;* Gath, *a sting.*

NOGA, *to reach, to touch :* Aig, *at.*

NOTHAN, *to give, to place ; than* perhaps like Daignich, *establish.*

NEHEE, *lamenting :* Och, *alas.*

NOGAH, *to shine, to illuminate :* Gath, *a ray of light.*

Nohor, *a river :* Ruith, *flow.*

Nouzleem, *running waters; n* prefixed ; *ouz* like Uisge, uis-ge, *water.*

Noven, *a habitation; veh* like Both, *a hut.*

Neokoh, *groaning :* Eigh, *a cry ; earnest entreaty.*

Nokav, *an excavation ; n* prefixed; *k* prefixed ; *av* like Uamh, *a cave.*

Nevel, *a drum :* Buail, *strike.*

Nohar, *to brighten;* like Hebrew oor, *to illuminate;* like Gaelic Brath, *fire; b* omitted.

Nolo, *to accomplish :* Uile, *all.*

Nokhoun, *correct :* Eagnaidh, *correct.*

Nigas, *to exact;* nougais, *persecution;* Cis, *a tax* (is cis good Gaelic?).

Novakh, *to bark; vaih* like Focal, foc-al, *a word.*

Nikhmor, *shrivelled by fire; mor* like Brath, *fire.*

Nogad, *to declare :* Guth, *a voice.*

Nogain, *to sing;* nogan, *to play upon an instrument;* negeenoh, *melody :* Can, say, *sing* (hence Latin cano).

Nokhar, no-khar, *to discern :* Cridhe, *the heart* (figuratively for the seat of mind).

Nokhath, no-khath, *to penetrate :* Gath, *a dart.*

Nomas, n-omas, *to melt, to dissolve; om* like Abh, *water; bh* to *m.*

Naar, *a youth, a lad;* naaroh, *a damsel :* Ur, *young.*

THIRD GROUP.

Negdee, *before me;* neged, *to reject :* An aghaidh, *opposite, against.*

Noham, *to bellow :* perhaps like Fuaim, *a noise; n* prefixed; *f* omitted.

SAMECH.

The fifteenth Hebrew letter.

Some Hebrew and Gaelic words are alike in meaning and sound, except that an initial *s* is either added in Hebrew, or omitted in Gaelic; either *s*, or *s* followed by a vowel-sound.

FIRST GROUP.

Words which begin with *s* in both languages.

Soor, *to separate :* Sreath, *a row* (to place in rows).

Sirioun, *a coat of mail :* Sreath, *a row* (material in rows).

Sookoh, sukkoh, sukoh, *a booth, shelter, tabernacle;* sikooth, *shelter;* sokhakh, *to protect;* sikhooth, *a protection;* sookhoh, *an awning;* sokhakh, sokakh, *to enclose, protect :* Sgiath, *a wing; a projection; shelter ; a shield.*

SAKHROH, SOUKHAIROH, *property, merchandise;* perhaps from being in sacks (compare with the rude word bagman): Sac, *a sack, a bag.*

SOUKHAIR, *a merchant,* from SAKHROH, *merchandise; sakh* or *soukh* like Gaelic Sac; *air* like fear (in composition—ar), *a man.*

SEKHEE, *sweepings;* perhaps like Sguab, *sweep.*

SEDER, *system, regularity:* Sreath, *a row.*

SELA, *a cleft in a rock:* perhaps like Sgoilt, *cleave.*

SECOND GROUP.

An initial *s* is either added in Hebrew, or omitted in Gaelic; either *s*, or *s* followed by a vowel-sound.

SOPHAR, *to cypher; to number; to relate;* SIPPAIR, *to account:* Abair, *say.*

SEVOKH, *a thicket; se* prefixed; *vo* like Fiodh, *wood.*

SOOTH, *a vesture:* Eid, *to clothe.*

SOOG, *to turn back:* perhaps like Ais, *back.*

SAIPHEL, *a bowl:* perhaps like Ubhall, *an apple* (in both there is the idea of roundness).

SOTAR, *to hide:* perhaps Tir, *earth* (suppose to cover with earth).

SOKHAV, *to drag away:* Gabh, *take.*

SOUPH, *the hinder end:* Ais, *behind.*

SOVAL, *to burden;* SAIVEL, *burden; el* like Uallach, uall-ach, *a burden.*

SOOR, *to depart:* Ruith, *run.*

SEKHARKHAR, *to beat quickly,* as the heart: *se* prefixed; *khar* repeated: *khar* like Crith, *shake;* also like cridhe, *the heart.*

SALOKH, *to pardon:* Logh, *pardon.*

SEAITH, *a swelling:* At, *a swelling.*

SOLAL, *to be raised up;* SOLOH, *to elevate;* SOLOOL, *a raised pathway;* SOULELOH, *a rampart;* SOULOM, *a ladder:* Ailt, *high.*

SOKHAL, *to become wise:* Ciall, *sense.*

SOKHAL, *to act foolishly:* perhaps As, *out of;* ciall, *sense.*

SAR, *a ruler;* SORAR, *to rule:* perhaps Ard, *high;* or sreath, *a rank, a row;* sreathaich, *arrange.*

SOROH, *rebelliously:* perhaps Ar, *fight.*

SOVAV, *to surround; s* prefixed; *ov* like Uim, *around; m* to *v.*

SOKHOR, so-khor, *a place for traffic:* Creic, *sell.*

SOLAPH, so-laph, *to bend:* Lub, *bend.*

SELA, se-la, *a rock:* Lia, *a stone.*

SOKAL, so-kal, *to stone, to remove stones;* SOKAL, so-kal, *to stone, to pelt:* Clach, *a stone.*

A conjecture is offered for the consideration of the reader. Is Hebrew initial *s* sometimes interchangeable or commutable with Celtic initial *c* or *g*? See the fourth group under the letter shin. I have looked under the letter zain for similar instances, but none have occurred to me. See the fourth group under the letter tsade.

SELA, *a rock:* perhaps akin to Clach, *a stone;* or lia, *a stone; se* prefixed.

SOMAKH, som-akh, *to support:* Cum, *hold.*

SEER, *a pot, a pan:* Cro, *anything round.*

AYIN.

The sixteenth Hebrew letter. The sound of this letter is not known with certainty. It has sometimes been represented by *g;* sometimes at the beginning of a word by *gn,* and at the end of a word by *ng.* In some works, in writing Hebrew in English letters, it is passed over altogether. In some works, where Hebrew is given in English letters, this letter is given in the Hebrew character. The way of representing it here is that followed by Aaron Pick in his *Bible-Student's Concordance;* it is here represented sometimes by *o,* sometimes by *a,* or *i, e,* or *u.*

Words which in Hebrew begin with ayin, and in Gaelic with a vowel.

OOR, *to start quickly, to awake:* Eirich, eir-ich, *rise.*

OLOH, *to ascend;* OLOUTH, *ascending;* ALLEEYOH, *an ascent;* ALLIYOH, *an upper room;* OLAZ, *to exult, to rejoice;* AL, *upon;* OULOH, *ascension* (a burnt-offering): Ailt, *high.*

EDAI (Syriac), ODATH (Syriac), ODOH (Chaldee), *to pass away:* Uidhe, *a step.*

OUD, *again:* Ath, *again.*

OUL, *an infant;* ELEM, *a lad;* OULAIL, *offspring;* OULAILOH, *a small grape, not full grown:* Al, *a brood; young of any kind.*

OULOM, *everlasting;* like Uile, *all;* am, *time.*

AVOOR, *old corn:* Arbhar, *corn.*

AROOGOH, *a raised bed in a garden:* perhaps Ard, *high.*

OUNEO, *delight;* ONAG, *to delight oneself;* Aoibhneach, *pleasant.*

OUL, *a burden:* Uallach, *a burden.*

IVVAID, *to surround;* ivv like Uim, *around;* aid like uidhe, *a step.*

UMMATH, *corresponding to, like:* Amhuil, amh-uil, *like.*

E

SECOND GROUP.

An initial vowel-sound is either added in Hebrew, or an initial vowel
is omitted in Gaelic.

AIVER, ai-ver, *over, beyond ;* OVAR, o-var; IBBAR, *to pass over:* Barr, *top.*

OPHOR, o-phor, *dust:* Bruth, *bruise.*

OVOOR, o-voor, *a grain of corn, produce:* Beir, *produce.*

OMAN, o-man, *to trust:* perhaps like Bun, *a foundation.*

OKOV, o-kov, *crooked;* OKAIV, *the heel,* from OKOV; or OKOV from OKAIV;
OKOUV, o-kouv, *unlevelled;* OKAV, *to supplant* (suppose to trip up);
OKAV, *to detain, restrain:* Cub, *bend.*

OKHAS, o-khas, *a tinkling ornament for the feet:* perhaps like Cos, *a foot.*

OPHI, o-phi, *a bough:* Fiodh, *wood.*

OUPHEL, ou-phel, *a hill, a mount;* OPHAL, o-phal, *to swell:* Meall,
a hill; m to *ph.*

AGVOH, *affection;* the *gv* like Caomh, *dear.*

OMOL, o-mol, *weariness:* Meil, *grind.*

OOPH, *to fly;* the *ph* like *f* in Fogair, *expel.*

AD, *unto:* Do, *to.*

AIDER, EDER, e-der, *a herd:* Treud, *a herd.*

OKAR, o-kar, *to root out, to disable:* Gearr, *cut.*

OTOH, o-toh, *to veil, to cover:* Tigh, *a house* (hence Latin tego).

OOGOL, oo-gol, *round:* Calbh, *a head.*

OVAD, *to serve;* AVOUDOH, *service:* Fo, *under;* the preposition turned
into a verb.

THIRD GROUP.

Perhaps at the beginning of the word, a consonant is either omitted in
Hebrew, or added in Gaelic. This is a conjecture offered for the
consideration of the reader. See the third group under the letter
aleph, the third group under the letter he, and the second group
under the letter yod.

OLEH, *a leaf:* Bileach, bil-each, *a leaf; b* omitted.

AIN, *a fountain;* see Hebrew MAAYON, *a fountain:* Buinne, *a pool in a
river; b* omitted.

OROH, *to strip, to bare:* Creach, *a raid, a foray; c* omitted.

ORATS, *to dread:* Crith, *to tremble; c* omitted.

ONEE, *poor, afflicted:* Caoin, *lament; c* omitted.

EER, *a city:* Cathair (the *t* silent), *a city; c* omitted.

OSAS, *to tread down:* Cos, *a foot; c* omitted.

OVOH, *to be bent down:* Cub, *bend; c* omitted.

OROOM, *cunning, subtle:* Crom, *crooked; c* omitted.

Innon, *to afflict*: Guin, *wound; g* omitted.

Orah, *a bare place*: Garbh, *rough, rugged; g* omitted.

Egloh, *a calf*: Laogh, *a calf; g* omitted; *e* prefixed.

Onoh, *to answer, to express;* ounoh, *a testimony;* onok, *to answer*: Fonn, *an air, a tune; f* omitted.

Aits, *a tree, wood, a piece of wood;* ait, *a reed-pen*: Fiodh, *wood; f* omitted.

Olam, *concealed*: Feile, *a covering; f* omitted.

Eer (Syriac), *a watcher*: Faire, *a watch, a guard; f* omitted.

Osoh, *to make, let grow, to do*: Fas, *grow; f* omitted.

Ain, ayin, *the eye*. A fanciful conjecture is offered for the consideration of the reader. I connect ain, *the eye*, with ain, *a fountain, a spring*, as on a hill-side a round spring may be likened to the eye of the hill. Ain, *a fountain*, is akin to the Gaelic Buinne, *a pool in a stream; b* omitted. Hence Latin fons.

Orakh, *to prepare, arrange*: Sreath, *a row; s* omitted.

FOURTH GROUP.

Egloh, *a calf*: perhaps like Gaelic Laogh, *a calf; g* prefixed; *e* prefixed. Laogh is said to be the most dificult word in Gaelic for a non-Gael to pronounce.

Arophel, *thick darkness;* aro like Ciar, *dark; c* omitted; *phel* like feile, *a covering*.

Am, *a people*: Aiteam, *a people, a tribe*.

PE.

The seventeenth Hebrew letter.

Some Hebrew and Gaelic words are alike in meaning and sound, except that an initial *p* is either added in Hebrew, or omitted in Gaelic; either *p*, or *p* followed by a vowel-sound.

FIRST GROUP.

Words which begin with *p* in both languages.

Porash, *to distinguish, to divide;* porad, *to part, to separate;* poroshoh, *a separate sum*: Pairt, *a part* (is pairt good Gaelic?).

Potsoh, *to open, to release;* pithkhoun, *a full opening;* pothak, *to open, to engrave;* pithgom, *a decree;* pithuk, *an engraving;* Pit, *a hollow*.

Petseeroh, *a file;* pouthoutn, *the socket in which the hinge moves* (in all these the idea is something hollow, as the sunk line on engraved metal); like Gaelic Pit, *a hollow*.

An initial *p* is either added in Hebrew, or omitted in Gaelic.

PAAM, *time, a time ;* Am, *time.*

POLAT, *to deliver ;* ol like Al, *young of any kind.*

POGA, POGASH, *to meet, to come to :* Aig, *at* (the preposition turned into a verb) ; or agaidh, *face.*

PENEEMEE, *inside :* Ann, *in.*

POTHAR, *to interpret :* perhaps Eadar, *between.*

PEKHOR, pe-khor (Syriac), *a potter :* Cre, *earth.*

Words which begin with *p* in Hebrew, and with *b* in Gaelic.

PHOREKH, *harshness, severity :* perhaps like Barr, *top* (overbearing).

PORATS, *to break forth ;* PORAKH, *to throw out or shoot :* Bruchd, *burst forth.*

POROSH, *a rider ;* perhaps like PUROH, *a branch ;* PERIS, *a claw :* Beir, *carry.*

PETHEN, *an asp ;* pe like Beach, *a bee.*

POROOR, *a swelling, increasing* as water boils over : Barr, *top ;* or mor, *great.*

PAIAIR, *an ornamental head-dress ;* PARTAIMEEM (Chaldee) *chiefs :* Barr, *top.*

POOR, *to break asunder, to disannul ;* POOROH, *a wine-press :* Bruth, *bruise, crush.*

PEAIR, *comely ;* POAR, *to beautify :* Briadha, *pretty ;* Lowland-Scotch, *braw.*

POAR, *to be praiseworthy :* perhaps like Mor, *great.*

PENNINAH, *a coral :* perhaps like Ban, *white.*

PATEESH, *an iron-hammer :* Bat, *strike.*

POROH, *a cow ;* po like Bo, *an ox.*

PILLAID, *to decide :* Beul, *the mouth.*

POROUR, *an iron pot :* the Hebrew for *iron* like Gaelic Brath, *fire ;* as fire was used in procuring or working iron.

PINNIAH, *a battlement :* Beinn, *a hill.*

POAL, *to work ;* in sound like Buail, *smite, thrash.*

PERAZAH, *a town :* Barr, *a height* (and applied to towns as these for security were built on heights).

PATH, *a bit, a piece, a morsel ;* like Hebrew PE, *a mouth ;* like Gaelic Bid (obs.), *nip, pinch ;* bideag, *a morsel.*

POKAKH, *to see ;* POKAD, *to review :* Beachd, *vision.*

FOURTH GROUP.

Words which begin with *p* in Hebrew, and with *f* in Gaelic.

POTHAL, *to spin, to twist :* Fill, *fold.*

PAAMON, *a bell :* perhaps like Fuaim, *noise.*

POSOH, *to spread itself, to increase :* Fas, *grow.*

POSHAT, posh-at, *to strip, to plunder :* Fas, *lay waste.*

FIFTH GROUP.

Words which begin with *p* in Hebrew, and with *m* in Gaelic.

POLAKH, *to grind, to powder :* Moil, *grind.*

PELE, PHELE, *wonderful ;* POLO, *to be wondered at ;* PELEEOII, *a wonder :* Miorbhuil, *a wonder,* from meur, *finger ;* and Beal, *the god Belus,* or *Bel.*

SIXTH GROUP.

PE, *the mouth ;* a little like Beul, *the mouth.*

POAR, *to open the mouth wide ;* like Hebrew PE; *pe* like Gaelic Abair, a-bai-r, *speak :* also like aber, *the mouth of a river.*

PARDAIS, *paradise, ornamental pleasure-ground :* perhaps like Briadha, *pretty ;* ais (obs.), *a covert.*

Is it the case that Hebrew initial *p* sometimes corresponds to Celtic initial *t,* as in the three following?

PONOH, *to turn :* Tionndaidh, tionn-daidh, *turn.*

POON, *to pine away :* Tana, *thin.*

PAR, *a bull ·* Tarbh, *a bull.*

TSADE.

The eighteenth Hebrew letter.

Some Hebrew and Gaelic words are alike in meaning and sound, except that either the Hebrew prefixes *ts,* or the Gaelic omits *ts* at the beginning of a word ; either *ts,* or *ts* followed by a vowel-sound.

Some Hebrew words beginning with *ts* are like Gaelic words beginning with *t.*

Some Hebrew words beginning with *ts* are like Gaelic words beginning with *s.*

FIRST GROUP.

In Hebrew the word begins with *ts,* and in Gaelic with *t* or *d.*

TSOOTH, *to set on fire ;* TSIYOH, *a dry waste or barren place :* Teas, *heat ;* teo, teodh, *hot.*

TSORAPH, *to refine, purify* (suppose to wash) ; the *or* perhaps like Doir, *water.*

Tsour, tsoor, *a rock, a stone, a flint;* tseer, *an image of stone:* Torr, *a hill;* or sgor, *a rock.*

At the beginning of a word, *ts* is either added in Hebrew, or omitted in Gaelic; either *ts,* or *ts* followed by a vowel-sound: about fourteen instances.

Tsolakh, ts-ol-akh, *to advance, to prosper;* ol like Al, *nourish, grow;* or ailt, *high.*

Tsophan, tso-phan, *to conceal:* Bun, *a foundation.*

Tsadeek, tsa-deek, *just, righteous;* tsedekh, tse-dekh, *righteousness:* Deagh, *good.*

Tsovar, tso-var, *to heap up:* Barr, *top;* or beir, *carry.*

Tsoak, ts-oak, *to call out;* tseokoh, ts-eokoh, *a loud cry;* tsokhakh, ts-okh-akh, *to laugh incredulously:* Eigh, *a cry, a shout.*

Tsohal, *to shout for joy:* Iolach, *a shout.*

Tsoeer, ts-oeer, *young, small:* Ur, *young.*

Tseer, tsee-r, *an express;* the r like Ruith, *run.*

Tsoad, ts-oad, *to march, to step;* tsaad, *a step;* tsood, *to hunt, to pursue;* tsoyid, *venison, game:* Uidhe, *a step, a journey.*

Tsouphar, tsou-phar, *morning (early):* Brath, *fire;* the fire in the east.

In Hebrew the word begins with *ts,* and in Gaelic with *s;* the sound of an initial *t* is either added in Hebrew, or omitted in Gaelic: six instances.

Tsorar, *to oppress;* tsoroh, *oppression;* tsourair, *an oppressor:* Saraich, sar-aich, *oppress.*

Tsourair, tsour-air, *an oppressor,* from tsoroh; *tsour* like Saraich, sar-aich, *oppress;* air like fear (in composition ar), *a man.*

Tsail, *a projection:* Sail, *a heel.*

Tseer, *fashion, fashioned:* Sreath, *a row, a line.*

Tsekheeakh, *exposed to the sun:* Seac, *dry.*

Some Hebrew words beginning with *ts* are like Gaelic words beginning with *sg.* Is this a case when Hebrew *s* is commutable with Celtic *g*? See the third group under the letter samech.

Tsail, *a shade;* tsolal, *shaded;* tselem, *a shadow:* Sgail, *a shade.*

Tsour, tsoor, *a rock, a stone, a flint;* tsoraath, *leprosy;* tsoroa, *leprous* (from the roughness of the skin); tseer, *an image of stone:* Sgor, *a rock;* also like torr, *a hill.*

A conjecture is offered for the consideration of the reader. Is it the case that at the beginning of a word, Hebrew *ts* sometimes corresponds to Gaelic initial *c* or *g*, as in the following?

TSEETS, *a shining plate of metal:* Gath, *a ray of light.*
TSOHAR, *an aperture for light :* Cro, *the eye of a needle.*
TSOMEED, tsom-eed, *a fastening :* Cum, *hold.*
TSIPPOH, *to overlay, to cover :* Cab, *a head.*
Also see the third group under the letter tov.

KOPH.

The nineteenth Hebrew letter—koph or quoph. Sometimes represented by *q* or *qu ;* here represented by *k.*

Some Hebrew and Gaelic words are alike in meaning and sound, except that either the Hebrew prefixes *k,* or the Gaelic omits an initial *c* or *g ;* either *k,* or *k* followed by a vowel-sound.

Some Hebrew and Gaelic words are alike in meaning and sound, except that an initial *s* is either omitted in Hebrew, or added in Gaelic ; as Hebrew KOOT, KEE, like Gaelic sgeith; Hebrew KAIN like Gaelic sgian.

Words which begin with *k* in Hebrew, and with *c* or *g* in Gaelic.

KOOM, *to establish ;* KOUMETS, *a handful :* Cum, *hold, withhold ; hold as in the hand.*
KILLAIL, *to esteem lightly ;* KOLAL, *to lighten:* perhaps Caol, *little, small.*
KOON, *to lament :* Caoin, *lament.*
KORO, *to call ;* KORO, *to be called, named;* KORATS, *to taunt;* KERUEEM, *the invited :* Gaoir, *noise.*
KORATS, *to nip, to pinch :* perhaps Gearr, *cut.*
KOUL, *a voice, noise ;* KOULOUTH, *a loud voice, thunder :* Glaodh, *call.*
KEREN, *a horn ;* KEREN, *a projecting corner ; a corner ;* KARNO (Chaldee), *a flute, cornet, horn:* Corn, *a horn, a trumpet;* corr, *a horn;* corran, *a point of land reaching far into the sea.*
KORAV, *to bring near :* perhaps like Cior (obs.), *the hand.*
KOSHAV, *to attend :* perhaps like Cos, *a foot.*
KARDOUN, *an axe ;* KORA, *to rend asunder :* Gearr, *cut.*
KARKAR, *to root out ; kar* repeated : Gearr, *cut.*
KOUROH, *a beam of a house;* a little like Crann, *a beam.*
KUBOH, *the stomach :* perhaps like Gabh, *receive* (the receptacle).
KOURAKH, *bold :* Garbh, *harsh, haughty.*

Konoh, *to buy*; kinyon, *a purchase*; Coannaich, *to buy.*

Keoroh, *a dish*; kaaroh, *a deep dish*: Cro, *anything round*; coire, *a hollow.*

Keer, *a well*: Cro, *a circle.*

Koram, *to cover, skin over*; a little like Croic, *the skin.*

Kotsar, *to shorten*; *kot* like Cutach, cut-ach, *short*; cutaich, *to shorten*; Lowland-Scotch, *cutty.*

Kerev, *inside, within* : Cridhe, *the heart.*

Kova, *to demand with authority*: Gabh, *take.*

Kov, *a measuring-line*: Caball, cab-all, *a rope.*

Koras, *to bend*: Car, *a turn.*

Kouts, *a thorn*: Gath, *a sting.*

Kotseh, *an end, a corner*: perhaps like Gath, *a sting, a point.*

Koloun, *contempt*: perhaps like Cul, *the back.*

Kan, *a nest*; konan, *to make a nest.* See gan, *a garden*; gonan, *to enclose.* Under the letter kheth, see khonoh, *to encamp*: under the letter kaph, see koon, *to erect, to establish*; kan, *a basis*; konas, konash, *to gather into a place of security.* Also see makhaneh, *a camp.* Of all these the idea is an enclosure. Also see tekhoonoh, *establishment, estate, property*; tikhain, *to ordain*; tikhoun, *established.* All these Hebrew words are akin to each other, and to the Gaelic Comhnuidh, comhn-uidh, *a dwelling*; an comhnuidh, *continually.*

SECOND GROUP.

An initial *k*, or this sound is either added in Hebrew, or omitted in Gaelic; either *k*, or *k* followed by a vowel-sound.

Kohal, *to assemble*; kohol, *an assembly*; kouheleth, *a collector.* Under the letter kaph, see kohal, *to assemble*; kohol, *an assembly*; koul, *all things, everything*; kol, *all*; koloh, *to complete*: under the letter kheth, see khail, *an army.* All these Hebrew words are akin to each other, and to the Gaelic Uile, *all.*

Koor, *to cause to spring up*: Eirich, eir-ich, *rise.*

Kor, *cold*; kerakh, *a clear stone*; *ice*: Reodh, *freeze.*

Kodar, *to darken*; kitreen, *obscure things*; koudair, *obscure*: Dorch, *dark.*

Koton, *little*: Tana, *thin, small.*

Kino, *envy*: Tnu, *envy.*

Kovar, *to bury*; *var* like Barr, *a top* (a heap).

Koshav, *to attend*: Ais, *behind.*

Korouv, *near, at hand*: Roi, *before.*

An initial *s* is either omitted in Hebrew, or added in Gaelic.

KOOT, *to loathe;* KEE, *to vomit :* Sgeith, *to vomit.*

KAIN, *a weapon with a long handle :* Sgian, *a knife.* Under the letter kaph, see Hebrew KOHOH, *dim,* like Gaelic sgiath, *a shade;* Hebrew KONOPH, kon-oph, *a wing,* like Gaelic sgiathan, *a little wing :* also see Hebrew GOLOH, *to reveal,* like Gaelic sgeul, *a tale;* instances where *s* is similarly treated.

RESH.

The twentieth Hebrew letter. Gaelic *r* is called rius, *the alder-tree.*

Some Hebrew words beginning with *r* are in meaning and sound like Gaelic words beginning with *c* or *g*; an initial *c* or *g*, or this sound, being either omitted in Hebrew, or added in Gaelic; either *c* or *g*, or one of these followed by a vowel.

Words which begin with *r* in both languages.

ROKA, *to beat out, to extend, to expand;* ROKAK, *to draw forth :* Ruig, *reach, extend.*

ROVOH, *to satiate with moisture, or by watering the ground;* ROOTS, *to run;* ROTS, *a runner;* ROHAT, *a trough, a channel;* RODAPH, *to pursue;* REER, *saliva;* REER, *juice, fluid;* ROUK, *saliva;* ROHAKH, *to spit :* Ruith, *run, flow.*

RESHOUN, *first;* ROUSH, *a chief, a head;* RAV, *a chief;* ROZOUN, *a prince :* Roi, *before.*

RINNOH, *a shout;* RONAN, *to sing;* RONOH, *to sound, to sing;* RONNAN, *to shout :* Rann, *a poem;* oran, *a song.*

ROV, *much;* RAV, *abundance;* ROKHAV, *to enlarge;* ROVOV, ROVAV, *to multiply;* ROVOH, *satiety, fulness :* Ro, *very, much, exceedingly.*

ROVOH, *satiety, fulness;* ro like Ro, *much;* voh like biadh, *food.*

RABHEEM, *a multitude, many :* Ro, *much.* Hebrew AM, *people :* perhaps like Gaelic Aiteam, *people.*

An initial *r* either added in Hebrew, or omitted in Gaelic.

REDEED, *a robe :* Eid, *clothe.*

RAK, *but :* Ach, *but.*

A conjectural affinity is offered for the consideration of the reader : an initial *c* or *g*, or this sound, is either omitted in Hebrew, or added in Gaelic.

Roal, *to be giddy, to stagger;* rogaz, *to tremble;* rotsats, *to chatter;* raash, *trembling; an earthquake;* road, raad, *trembling;* rogash, *to rage, to storm* (to shake with rage); rokhaph, *to flutter;* roash, *to bluster, to shake;* raayoun, *intentions, thoughts :* Cridhe, *the heart* (figuratively the seat of mind).

Rovats, *to crouch down;* rophats, *to tread down :* Crub, *crouch.*

Resheth, *a net;* rukamtee, *embroidered :* Car, *a turn.*

Raia, raiah, *a friend;* reooth, *a companion;* roa, *to be social*; raioh, *to befriend :* Car, *a friend;* car, *friendly.*

Reek, *empty;* reek, *to empty;* raikom, *empty, in vain;* rokakh, *to empty :* Creach, *plunder, pillage.*

Roov, *hunger :* Ocras, *hunger; c* omitted, *o* omitted.

Rotsoh, *to be willing;* rotsoun, *acceptance, will;* reooth (Chaldee), *pleasure :* Gradh, *affection.*

Rom, *great :* Garbh, *large; g* omitted; *bh* to *b*; *b* to *m.*

Revooth, *greatness :* Garbh, *huge,* &c.

Rosham, *to note;* the *r* perhaps like Gearr, *cut;* or garbh, *rough;* or sgriobh, *write; g* omitted.

If any one were to say that Gaelic sgriobh was the daughter of Latin scribo, he might be told that scribo was the daughter of Gaelic garbh. It is not here admitted that sgriobh is from scribo.

Rooa, *to shout :* Gaoir, *noise.*

FOURTH GROUP.

An initial letter is either omitted in Hebrew, or added in Gaelic.

Reev, *to contend;* reev, *an opponent;* reev, *a controversy :* Ar, *fight; a* omitted.

Roa, *to break in pieces;* reseeseem, *ruins :* Bris, *break; b* omitted.

Rokhash, *to rush;* rekhesh, *a swift animal, a dromedary;* rakhov, *a swift rider, a chariot-driver;* rokad, *to dance, jump;* rekhev, *a chariot;* rekhev, *the upper mill-stone* (the rider); reek, *to empty, to pour out abundantly :* Bruchd, *rush forth; b* omitted.

Rokhav, *breath;* rooakh, *spirit, breath, wind :* perhaps akin to Bruchd, *rush forth, belch; b* omitted.

Rokav, *to rot;* a little like Breoth, *to rot.*

In the four words below, an initial *f* either omitted in Hebrew, or added in Gaelic.

Rooh, *to feed;* roueh, *a feeder of a flock :* Four, *grass.*

Roupha, *a physician, a healer :* perhaps *r* like Fearr, *better.*

Rogash, *to rage;* rougez, *anger :* Fearg, *anger;* or crith, *shake* (with rage).

RoGAZ, *to shake with rage:* Fearg, *anger; f* omitted; or crith, *shake* (with rage).

Ro, ROOH, ROUA, *evil;* ROOA, *to do evil;* ROSHO, *a bad man;* ROSHA, *to act wickedly:* Droch, *bad; d* omitted in Hebrew, or added in Gaelic.

SHIN or SIN.

The twenty-first Hebrew letter.

Some Hebrew and Gaelic words are alike in meaning and sound, except that either the Hebrew prefixes shin or sin, or the Gaelic omits an initial *s;* either *s,* or *s* followed by a vowel-sound.

FIRST GROUP.

Words which begin with *sh* or *s* in Hebrew, and with *s* in Gaelic.

SHOOTH, SHEETH, *to set, to place;* SHUTH, *a foundation:* Suidh, *sit;* suidhich, *set, place.*

SHEVETH, *a seat;* she like Suidh, *sit.*

SHOKOH, *to quiet, to still:* Socraich, soc-raich, *appease, assuage.*

SHIRYOUN, *a coat of mail:* Sreath, *a row* (pieces of metal in rows).

SOURAKHATH, *a display:* Sreath, *spread.*

SEREEKOUTH, *combed:* Sreath, *a row.*

SEROD, *a covering:* Sreath, *spread* (the idea is something spread).

SHOGO, *to wander:* Seachran, seach-ran, *to wander.*

SHAKHATH, *destruction;* SHOKHAT, *to slay* as a sacrifice: Sgath, *consume, destroy.*

SUKKAH, *a covering, a tabernacle;* SOUKHOH, *a bough;* SOKHAKH, *to protect, to enclose:* Sgiath, *a wing, shelter, protection, shade.*

SAKEEN, *a knife:* Sgian, *a knife.*

SHOROH (Syriac), *to let loose;* SORAD, *to escape:* Saor, *free.*

SHAINOH, *sleep:* Suain, *sleep.*

SHAISH, *six:* Se, *six.*

SHAIREETH, *service;* SHORATH, *to minister, to attend:* Naothair, *work.*

SAK, *a sack:* Sac, *a sack.*

SHEKETS, SHIKOOTS, *a detestable thing;* SHOKATS, *to detest* (see KEE, KOOT): Sgeith, *to vomit.*

SHELAKH, *a dart;* perhaps akin to Sealg, *to hunt.*

THIRD GROUP.

An initial *sh* or *s* is either added in Hebrew, or omitted in Gaelic; either *s,* or *s* followed by a vowel-sound; about fifty-nine instances.

SHEKHAN, *a resting-place;* SHOKHAN, *to rest, to dwell;* SHOKHAIN, *an inhabitant.* See MAKHANEH, *a camp.* Under the letter kheth, see

KHONOH, *to encamp:* under the letter kaph, see KOON, *to erect;*
KAN, *a basis;* KONAS, KONASH, *to gather into a place of security:*
under the letter koph, see KAN, *a nest;* KONAN, *to make a nest.*
Also see GAN, *a garden;* GONAN, *to enclose;* MEKHOUNOH, *a foundation, a base;* TEKHOUNOSH, *establishment, estate, property;* TIKHOUN,
established. Of KHONOH, MEKHANEH, KONAN, and GONAN, the idea
is an enclosure. All these Hebrew words are akin to each other,
and to the Gaelic Comhnuidh, comhn-uidh, *a dwelling;* an
comhnuidh, *continually.*

SHORATS, *to creep:* perhaps like Ruith, *run.*

SHOVEH, sh-ov-eh, *alike, equal;* ov like Amhuil, amh-uil, *like.*

SHOLAT, sh-ol-at, *to rule;* ol like Ailt, *high.*

SEEER, seee-r, *mist, vapour, small rain:* Ruith, *flow, run.*

SEER, see-r, *hoar-frost;* the r like Reodh, *freeze.*

SOGAV, so-gav, *to exalt:* Cab, *head.*

SHOVAR, sho-var, *to break, to break forth;* var like Bruth, *bruise, break;*
or bruchd, *burst forth.*

SHEVER, she-ver, *a shivering, a breaking:* Bruth, *bruise, break.*

SHO-VAKH, *to applaud:* Beuc, *utter a sound.*

SHOKHOUR, sho-khour, *black:* Ciar, *black.*

SHOAL, sh-oal, *to ask;* SHEAILOH, *a petition:* Iolach, iol-ach, *a shout.*

SHOKHAV, sho-khav, *to lie, to repose:* Cub, *bend.*

SHEKOKEEM, she-khok-eem, *skies:* perhaps like Cuach, *a cup;* the cup
inverted.

SAIKHEL, *intelligence;* SOKHAL, *to act prudently;* SIKAIL, *to act discreetly;*
khel like Ciall, *sense.*

SHOKHAL, sho-khal, *to deprive:* Caill, *lose.*

SHEGER, she-ger, *offspring, increase of cattle;* ger like Greigh, *a herd.*

SOVO, so-vo, *to satisfy with food;* vo like Biadh, *food.*

SHOMEER, sho-meer, *a diamond or other precious stone;* meer like Brath,
fire (from its sparkling).

SHAIVET, shai-vet, *a staff, a sceptre;* vet like Bat, *a staff.*

SHAPHREER, sha-phreer, *a covering for a throne;* phreer like Barr,
top.

SHOPHAKH, sho-phakh, *to pour out:* perhaps like Beuc, *roar, bellow*
(pour out sound).

SHAILOH, sh-ailoh, *a descendant, offspring:* Al, *the young of any animal.*

SOKAL, so-kal, *to stone, to pelt;* SOKAL, so-kal, *to stone, to remove stones;*
cal like Clach, *a stone.*

SEAITH, s-eaith, *a swelling:* At, *a swelling.*

SHOMAR, sh-omar, *to observe;* omar like Amhairc, *see.*

Sheor, sh-eor, *a remnant;* shoar, *to cause to remain;* soreed, *remainder;* shaiair, *a remnant :* Iar, *behind.*

Shotaph, sh-ot-aph, *to overflow; ot* like Ad (obs.), *water.*

Shad, sh-ad, *refreshing moisture; ad* like Ad, *water.*

Sar, *a ruler :* perhaps like Ard, *high.*

Soton, *a hinderer, Satan :* perhaps like Ais, *back, backward; ton* like duine, *a man.*

Sooakh, *to utter :* seeakh, *utterance;* beeakh, *to speak;* shooa, *a cry for help;* shoag, *to roar;* shooh, *to make a noise :* Eigh, *a cry.*

Shetai, she-tai, *both :* Da, *two.*

Shever, she-ver, *false; ver* like Fiar, *wicked, perverse.*

Shoov, shoo-v, *to revoke; shoo* either *sh* prefixed simply, or like Gaelic Ais, *back; v* like focal, foc-al, *a word;* also like beuc, *utter a sound* (like Latin voco).

Souvokh, sou-vo-kh, *a thicket; vo* like Fiodh, *wood.*

Shovar, sho-var, *to bargain, to sell :* perhaps like Margadh, mar-gadh, *a market.*

Shotak, sho-tak, *to still, to quiet :* Tachd, *choke.*

Sotoh, so-toh, *to deviate, to go aside :* Taobh, *a side.*

Shoushan, sh-oush-an, *a rose,* perhaps a red rose; *oush* like Hebrew aish, *fire;* like Gaelic Teas, *heat.*

Shouham, *an onyx stone; a carbuncle; a glittering stone;* like Hebrew aish, *fire; ai* omitted; like Teas, *heat;* teo, *hot.*

Shozaph, sh-oz-aph, *to shine; oz* like Hebrew aish, *fire;* like Gaelic Teas, *heat.*

Sholaim, sh-olai-m, *whole;* sholam, sh-ola-m, *to complete;* shillaim, sh-illai-m, *to complete :* Uile, *all.*

Shouvch, sh-ouv-ch, *to balance, to equal; ouv* like Amhuil, amh-uil, *like.*

Shaatoh, sh-aatoh, *progressing :* Uidhe, *a step.*

Sotoh, s-otoh, *to go astray; to avoid :* Taobh, *a ride;* or uidhe, *a step.*

Shonoh, *to repeat :* perhaps like Ais, *back;* fonn (in composition onn), *a tune, an air.*

Shephel, she-phel, *an elevated place : phel* like Meall, *a hill; m* to *ph.*

FOURTH GROUP.

A conjectural affinity is offered for the consideration of the reader. Some Hebrew words are in meaning and sound like Gaelic words, except that in Hebrew the initial letter is shin or sin, and in Gaelic c or g. See the third group under the letter samech. I

have looked under the letter zain for similar instances, but none
have occurred to me. See the fourth group under the letter tsade.

SHOPHAL, shoph-al, *to debase :* Cab, *head.*

SOOM, *to set, to place ;* SOMAKH, *to support :* Cum, *hold.*

SHOOV, *to turn, to return :* Cam, *bent.*

SHOOR, *to watch :* Caithris, *a watching.*

SORAKH, *to interweave, to traverse :* Car, *a turn.*

SHEPHOH, *abundance :* Cob, *plenty.*

SHOOP, *to crush :* Caob, *strike with clods.*

SHOOR, *an ox :* Crodh, *cattle.*

SHOULAYIM, *the skirts of a garment :* Cul, *behind.*

SHOVOH, *to capture :* Gabh, *take.*

SAPH, *a basin :* Gabh, *take, receive.*

SHAIN, *a tooth :* perhaps akin to Geinn, *a wedge.*

SHEER, *a song ; singing ;* SHOR, *a singer :* Gaoir, *noise.*

SAIOR, *hair ;* SOEER, *a hairy, rough goat:* Garbh, *rough.*

SHAAROOROH, *horrible :* Garbh, *rough, boisterous ;* the sound repeated.

SHOKAL, sho-kal, *to weigh :* perhaps like Clach, *a stone.* (See mishkol.)

SHOROV, *a dry place,* a barren spot : Garbh, *rough, wild,* not cultivated.

TOV.

The twenty-second Hebrew letter.

Some Hebrew and Gaelic words are alike in meaning and sound,
except that either an initial *t* is added in Hebrew, or omitted in
Gaelic ; either *t,* or *t* followed by a vowel-sound.

FIRST GROUP.

Words beginning with *t* in Hebrew, and with *d* or *t* in Gaelic.

TAIL, *a hill, a mount ;* TOLOUL, *raised up ;* TAIL, *a heap of ruins* (a heap);
TOLOH, *to hang :* Tula, *a hill.*

TANOOR, *a furnace :* Teine, *fire.*

TOR, *an ox :* Tarbh, *a bull.*

TANNEEN, *a serpent :* perhaps Tana, *thin, slim, slender.*

TOM, TOMEEM, *perfect ;* TOMAM, *to make perfect :* Teoma, *correct.*

TAKHTECHO, *under it :* Tigh, *a house.*

TOUAR, *form, shape :* Dreach, *form, shape.*

TIKVOH, *hope ;* TOUKHELETH, *hope ;* tik like Dochas, doch-as, *hope.*

TARBEETH, *increase :* Toradh, *fruit.*

TOUREN, *a mast ; a steeple ;* like Torr, *a hill* (the idea being something
high).

TEROOMOH, *an oblation :* perhaps like Thoir, *give.*

TENOOOH, *determination :* Teann, *firm.*

THOU, *a buffalo :* Damh, *an ox.*

To, *a chamber :* Tigh, *a house.*

TEHOUM, *profound, deep :* Tamh, *rest, quiet.* From tamh come these river-names—Tay, Thames, Tavy, Tamar; the idea being a smoothly-flowing river.

TOUR, *to reconnoitre, explore, search :* Dearc, *see.*

TEOUMEEM, *twins :* Da, *two.*

TOOH, *to wander, to go astray :* perhaps like Taobh, *a side.*

SECOND GROUP.

An initial *t* is either added in Hebrew, or omitted in Gaelic; either *t,* or *t* followed by a vowel-sound.

TIPHERETH, ti-phereth, *comely :* Briadha, *pretty ;* hence Lowland-Scotch *braw.*

TEVEL, te-vel, *confusion :* perhaps like Buail, *strike, smite.*

TEVOONOH, te-voon-oh, *understanding ;* voon like Mein, *mind.*

TAANOUG, t-annoug, *delight :* Aoibhneach, *pleasant.*

TIGROH, ti-groh, *an attack :* perhaps like Gearr, *cut.*

TEVOOSOTH, te-voos-oth, *treading down ;* voos like Greek pous; Latin pes; Gaelic Cos, *a foot ; c* to *p* and *v.*

TOKA, to-ka, *to blow a horn or trumpet ; ka* like Guth, *a voice.*

TEHILLOH, t-chilloh, *praise :* Iolach, iol-ach, *a shout.*

TEPHILLOH, te-philloh, *prayer :* perhaps like Beul, *the mouth.*

TENOOOH, *a prohibition :* Neo, *not.*

TEMOONOH, t-em-oonoh, *a resemblance :* perhaps *em* like Amhuil, amh-uil, *like.*

TOTYAH, *a going out :* Uidhe, *a step.*

THAKHANOUNEEM, *supplication ; akh* like Eigh, *a cry, earnest entreaty.*

TEKHOONOH, *establishment, estab, property ;* TIKHOUN, *established.* See MAKHANEH, *a camp.* Under the letter kheth, see KHONOH, *to encamp :* under the letter kaph, see KOON, *to erect ;* KAN, *a basis ;* KONAS, KONASH, *to gather into a place of security :* under the letter koph, see KAN, *a nest ;* KONAN, *to make a nest.* Also see OAN, *a garden ;* GONAN, *to enclose.* Also see SHEKHAN, *a resting-place ;* SHOKHAN, *to rest ;* SHOKHAIN, *an inhabitant.* Of KHONOH, KAN, and OAN, the idea is an enclosure. All these Hebrew words are akin to each other, and to the Gaelic Comhnuidh, comhn-uidh, *a dwelling ;* an comhnuidh, *continually.*

THEEROUSH, th-eer-oush, *new wine :* Ur, *new;* uisge, *water ;* from uisge comes whiskey.

THIRD GROUP.

A conjectural affinity is offered for the consideration of the reader. Some Hebrew and Gaelic words are alike in meaning and sound, except that in Hebrew the initial letter is *t;* in Gaelic, *c* or *g.*

TOUR, *a turn :* Car, *a turn.*

TAAVOH, *an object of desire :* Caomh, *dear.*

TOV, *a mark;* TOVOH, *to mark;* TABAATH, *a seal, a ring;* TOUPH, *a tabret, drum, timbrel :* Caob, *strike.*

TEOLOH, *a conduit, a trench :* Caol, *narrow.*

TOMAKH, *to support, to sustain :* Cum, *hold.*

TERIPH, *an image :* Cre, *earth.*

TAALUMOUTH, *hidden things :* Ceil, *hide.*

TOPHAS, *to lay hold of :* Gabh, *take.*

TEROOOH, *a sound of a trumpet :* Gaoir, *noise.*

THAAR, *a sharp instrument, a razor :* Gearr, *cut.*

Also see the fifth group of words under the letter tsade. As a young child learning to speak often uses *t* instead of *c,* as *I tome* for *I come,* some would be inclined to say that the people who used *c* instead of *t* were more advanced in mental culture, and in the use of the faculty of speech.

TOUR, *a row* (see under the letter teth, TOOR, *a row :* perhaps like Sreath, *a row; s* omitted; *t* prefixed.

———————

OMITTED.

In page 9. In Hebrew and Gaelic the verb has no present tense. The only Gaelic verb that has one is the verb Bi, *to be.* (*Stewart.*) In Hebrew and Gaelic there are only two genders, masculine and feminine ; no neuter gender.

ALEPH. This letter is here represented by *a, e, o,* or *u.*

OKHOO, *a pasture, a meadow :* like the Gaelic Acha, *a plain.*

(Acha is an important word, and enters into the composition of many names of places, as Auchinleck, &c.)

To the great relief of the reader, I now come to the end of this Essay. Although it is much larger than it was in 1840 and 1870, I venture to call this the Third Edition. In noting these signs of similarity, or supposed similarity, between the Hebrew and the Gaelic, I have not received any help from any quarter—printed or written matter, or conversation.

Hebrew has a way of prefixing a letter or a syllable to Hebrew words; thus KOON or KHONOH appear as TIKHOUN and SHEKHAN.

Has Gaelic a way of prefixing a letter or a syllable to Gaelic words? This exists to a very small extent. In thirty-six instances (or more), Gaelic prefixes a letter to a Gaelic word; in five cases (or more), Gaelic prefixes a syllable to a Gaelic word. Of the following pairs of Gaelic words the meaning is either the same, or somewhat similar:—Abh, tabh: abair, labhair: acha, faich: ar (kill), gearr: ar (plough), gearr: aom, cam: ais (a stronghold), caise (steepness): nig—as in aigeal, aigeann is like deoch: bun, spion: brigh, spairt: ceil, sgail: corrach, sgorrach: eirich, dirich: fal, speal: glaodh, sgal: glaodh, sgeul: geinn, sgain: garbh, sgriob: garbh, sgriobh: lan, slan: lar (a floor), blar (a level surface, a field): luchd (people), sliochd (a race, descendants), perhaps sliochd from siol (seed, progeny) and luchd; the *ochd* being a collective affix, from luchd: loch, slochd: mein, smuain: oileamh, foghluim: ros, gnos (pronounced gros): ruith, sruit: ruith, sruth: reic, ereic: rann, oran; rann, cronan: tarbh, storr: torr, stor: tir (earth), stur (dust, in Lowland-Scotch stour): uile (all), buileach (thoroughly).

The five cases where Gaelic prefixes a syllable to a Gaelic word are:—Falbh (go), siubhal, sin-bhal (travel): leus, solus: saighead, sai-ghead (an arrow), gath (an arrow, a dart): ruith (to flow, to run), gearrach (a flux): glaodh (call), focal, fo-cal (a word).

With reference to the above, some would be inclined to say that ar (to kill), and ar (to plough), need not be supposed to be akin to gearr. On the whole, it is to an extremely small extent that Gaelic has a way of prefixing a letter or a syllable to a Gaelic word. Within the last hundred years or so, any foreign words that have crept into the language never have any prefix given them : any tendency to change is in the direction of pronouncing indistinctly the last syllable of some words: in this way, a *d* or a *t* that ought to be sounded is made silent, and *h* is placed after it to show this.

Stewart, writing in the year 1801, complains that in some parts of the Highlands, from laziness, some words were pronounced not distinctly enough, and not as full as they were in other parts. (*Gaelic Grammar*, page 16.)

If some readers wish it, we may leave out the conjectural cases, and attend only to the others, and then even the most timid etymologist must admit that there is a wonderful amount of affinity between the Hebrew and the Celtic, or Keltic. The next consideration is, how to apply this to any historical purpose. Various questions may be asked, and it is much easier to ask them than to answer them. Are Hebrew and Celtic of equal antiquity? If not of equal antiquity, which is the more ancient? I do not know enough of the subject to be able to answer this. Some may say that the grammatical structure of Celtic is more elaborate and less simple than that of Hebrew, and that therefore Hebrew looks more ancient. But, on the other hand, it is impossible to say what its grammatical development might have been, if Hebrew had continued to be a spoken language till now, instead of ceasing * to be a living tongue perhaps twenty-four centuries ago.

If there was no direct connection between Hebrew and Celtic, did one link, that is, some other language, come in between? Or were there five or six links between, that is, as many languages? These inquiries I am glad to leave to be settled by others.

For the sake of some inquirers, it may be mentioned that interesting matter on philology may be found in Monboddo's Origin of Language, Brodie on Articulate Sounds, Barclay's Sequel to the Diversions of Purley, Prichard's Physical History of Mankind (1837), and Mr. Gladstone's Juventus Mundi (1869).

The darkness of early history may in some cases be lessened by the light of etymological research. " The similitude and derivation of languages afford the most indubitable proof of the traduction of nations, and the genealogy of mankind. They often add physical certainty to historical evidence, and often supply the only evidence of ancient migrations, and of the revolutions of ages, which left no written monuments behind them." (Dr. Sam. Johnson in a Letter to William Drummond, Life by Boswell, vol ii., page 38.)

---

* Hebrew appears to have varied but little in a period of one thousand years from Moses to Malachi. The old Hebrew became extinct as a living language about 500 B.C.; a thousand years afterwards, the Masoretic points were added to assist in its pronunciation. The Chaldee had superseded the Hebrew at the time of the captivity, and was gradually converted into the Syro-Chaldaic, which is called Hebrew in the New Testament. Thomas Young, M.D., in Article ' Languages,' Supplement to the Encyclopædia Britannica, 1824; and Miscellaneous Works 1 55 , vol. iii., page 521.

It is observed by Quintilian that:—Grammatice est ars, necessaria pueris, jucunda senibus, dulcis seorctorum comes, et quæ vel sola omni studiorum genere plus habet operis, quam ostentationis. Ne quis tanquam parva, fastidiat grammatices clementa, quia interiora velut sacri hujus adcuntibus, apparebit multa rerum subtilitas quæ non modo acuere ingenia puerilia, sed exercere altissimam quoque eruditionem ac scientiam possit. (Institutes of Oratory, i. 4.)

The relationship of the different branches of the human family is a part of Physiology (or Biology in the most correct meaning of this word), and so may be claimed to be within the wide area of Medical Investigation or Inquiry; and this relationship has to be traced by an examination of their languages.

The assertions of those who disbelieve the Bible account of the creation of man, have been in part answered by writers like Dr. Prichard and others, who have traced the links of language through the chain of the world's inhabitants.

The present attempt also is, as far as it goes, a small contribution towards the same end.

NOTE TO PAGE 59.

In the *Affinity of the Latin to the Celtic* (1840), I referred to what, about that time, was thought in some quarters, on that subject. Lieut.-Col. Vans Kennedy, H.E.I.C.S. (afterwards Major-General), had resided many years in India, and had occasion there to give much attention to the subject of languages. He wrote, *On the Origin and Affinity of Languages* (London : Longmans. 1827. Quarto). Also, *On Ancient and Hindoo Mythology* (London : Longmans. Quarto).

I have not the works to refer to, to be able to give the number of pages, but the reader will see that they are of considerable size, as each is published at two guineas and a half. In the former work, Vans Kennedy says that Greek and Latin have no affinity to the Celtic. My Essay was, as far as I know, the first attempt to inquire at any length into the subject. I gave proofs that there *was* affinity, and also that this affinity existed to a very considerable extent.

On this occasion (1872), on looking to see if anything has been said about any affinity between Hebrew and Celtic, I find (April, 1872) some remarks in Professor Max Müller's *Chips from a German Workshop* (London : Longmans. 1867. Vol. i., page 22). In common, I suppose, with all other persons, I have a great opinion of the talents and learning of Max Müller, although, when he refers to the Celtic, I am not always able to see the correctness of his views. (I here allude to an article on Cornish Antiquities in *Chips from a German Workshop*, vol. iii. (1870), page 267. There is not room in this place to quote it at length, but it seems to me to show a most transparent want of fairness when he is referring certain specimens of language and buildings to their source, whether Celtic, Roman, Saxon, or Norman.)

Max Müller speaks of the way of arranging the languages of the world in four divisions.

In the Indo-European division are Sanskrit, Persian, Celtic, Slavonic, Greek, Latin (and the four daughters of Latin, Italian, French, Spanish, and Portuguese); all the Teutonic languages of Europe; and English. "All these languages together form one "family, one whole, in which every member shares certain features in "common with all the rest, and is at the same time distinguished from "the rest by certain features peculiarly its own.

"The same applies to the Semitic family, which comprises, as its "most important members, the Hebrew of the Old Testament, the "Arabic of the Koran, and the ancient languages on the monuments "of Phenicia and Carthage, of Babylon and Assyria. These languages "again form a compact family, and differ entirely from the other "family, which we called Aryan or Indo-European." (*Chips*, i. p. 22.)

The reader is asked to compare the opinion given in the above extract, with the proofs here given of the existence of a very great affinity between Hebrew and Celtic.

May, 1872.

APPENDIX.

----

1. Illustrations of the Affinity of Latin to the Gaelic Language, or the Celtic of Scotland. Toronto, Upper Canada. Hugh Scobic. Printed by Hugh Scobic, at the office of the *British Colonist* Newspaper. 1840.

Two hundred and fifty copies printed. Published in July, 1840.

(Extracts, six or eight inches long, from the above were printed in twenty-nine successive numbers of the *Cuairtear nan Coillte* (Tourist of the Woods), a Gaelic weekly newspaper published at Kingston, Upper Canada, in 1841 and 1842. The *Cuairtear* began in December, 1840, and was continued for at least two years.)

2. Proofs of the Celtic Origin of a great part of the Greek Language; being a comparison of Greek with the Gaelic Language, or the Celtic of Scotland. Kingston, Upper Canada. Printed by John Creighton, at the office of the *Chronicle and Gazette* Newspaper. 1840.

Two hundred and thirty copies printed. Published in September, 1840. Although not mentioned in the title-page, at the end was given a short comparative vocabulary of Hebrew and Gaelic. The above two were published at 1s. 6d.

3. The Derivation of many Classical Proper Names from the Gaelic Language, or the Celtic of Scotland; being Part Third of an Inquiry into the Partly-Celtic Origin of the Greeks and Romans. Edinburgh: Adam and Charles Black; and Longman & Co., London. 1845. Printed at the University Press, Thistle Street, Edinburgh, by Stevenson & Co. Pp. 47. Price 1s. 6d.

Two hundred and fifty copies printed.

4. The Celtic Origin of a Great Part of the Greek and Latin Languages, and of many Classical Proper Names; being a comparison

of Greek and Latin with the Gaelic Language. Second Edition. Edinburgh: Maclachlan and Stewart; and Simpkin, Marshall, & Co., London. Printed by John Smith, Treville Street, Plymouth. 1870. Pp. 100. Three hundred and fifty copies printed. This was a second edition of the three essays mentioned above. The comparative vocabulary of Hebrew and Gaelic was printed as in 1840, and without any alteration. Price 2s. 6d.

5. On the Necessity for the Formation of the Scottish National Association for the Vindication of Scottish Rights. This was published in *Haszard's Gazette* (a weekly newspaper, Prince-Edward Island), of 30 November, 1853.

Forty copies struck off in pamphlet-form.

Also in the *Islander* (a weekly newspaper, Prince-Edward Island), of 9 December, 1853. One hundred copies struck off in pamphlet-form (seven pages).

Also in the Toronto *News of the Week*, of about 17 January, 1854.

In 1853 there was great need for the Scottish Rights Association; there is nearly as much in 1872. Some persons may ask, What connection is there between the Scottish Rights Association and Celtic matters? If the Society had continued its proceedings, it is likely that the Scotch Census of 1861 and 1871 would have been taken in a proper manner.

THE HIGHLAND SOCIETY OF CANADA

Is a Branch of the Highland Society of London. In 1844, it held its meetings at the town of Cornwall, on the left bank of the St. Lawrence, eighty-two miles above Montreal. The number of its honorary members was limited to twelve. On account of the *Celtic Origin of Greek and Latin* the Society, in 1844, made me an honorary member. An account of the Society, by Archibald John Macdonnell, of Greenfield, Canada, was published, in 1844, by Messrs. Armour and Ramsay, Montreal.

THE CENSUS OF SCOTLAND. 1871.

An Act of Parliament respecting the Census to be held in April is passed in the year previous. The wording of the Act is the same for the three divisions of the United Kingdom. In 1870 and 1871 the Home-Secretary was the Right Hon. Henry A. Bruce; the Lord Advocate, the Right Hon. George Young; the Registrar-General of Scotland, William Pitt Dundas, Esq. In the three Acts passed in 1870, there is no mention made of the Gaelic, Welsh, or Irish languages. Each Census-return is in the form of a Report addressed to the Home-Secretary. If the Welsh-language statistics had been omitted, some might have attributed this, and the omission of the Gaelic-language statistics, to some action, or want of action, on the part of the Home-Secretary. But as the Welsh-speaking inhabitants were numbered in 1871, there does not seem to be altogether a sufficient reason for this notion, and apparently those interested in Gaelic must attribute their disappointment (in the Gaelic-speaking inhabitants not being enumerated) to the Registrar-General at Edinburgh. Some persons then said that the language-statistics ought to be taken by themselves, and the expense of doing so deducted from the salary of the Scotch Registrar-General. In the Acts of Parliament ordering the Census, there ought to be distinct mention of the Gaelic, Welsh, Irish, and Manx languages. It is a matter too important to be left to chance, and to the caprice or indifference of whatever officials may happen to be in office at the time.

As it is the country that is at the expense of the Census being taken, the country has a right to require that it be taken in a proper manner. In May, 1870, the following was sent to the Home-Secretary : "To the Right Hon Henry A. Bruce, Secretary of State for the Home Department. The Memorial of the Committee of the General Assembly of the Free Church of Scotland, for the Highlands and Hebrides, Sheweth—That it is desirable, in taking the Census in 1871, that care should be taken to secure the accurate enumeration of the Gaelic-speaking population of Scotland ; that many important purposes, both social and educational, would be served by having such an enumeration ; that this was done in the case of the Irish-speaking population of Ireland in the last Census ; and that reasons equally weighty exist for having the same done in the case of Scotland. That one column in the Census-Schedule would secure the object, which should be to ascertain the number that can speak Gaelic. May it please Her Majesty's Government to take steps for the above purpose. In name and by authority of the Committee, (Signed,) THOMAS MACLAUCHLAN, Convener."

Registrar-General, George Graham, Esq.
Medical Superintendent of Statistics, William Farr, M.D.

THE WELSH LANGUAGE.

THE Preliminary Report on the Census states, that in 1871 they issued for Wales some schedules in Welsh. It is not mentioned how many in Welsh, and how many in English, nor how many Welsh schedules were used. The writer adds, that in 1881 they will perhaps not require to issue any schedules in Welsh. The Welsh Census, besides North and South Wales, includes the county of Monmouth, which in local situation, in race, and in language, is a part of Wales. There are about thirty Welsh periodical publications in Wales, America, and Australia. Remarks on the language and literature of Wales may be found in *Fraser's Magazine* for August, 1870, and for January, March, April, and June, 1871. If they had always noted the Welsh-language statistics at each Census since 1801, we should now have been able to see at one view, its condition at the eight ten-yearly periods. The results ascertained in 1871 have not yet (May, 1872, been published, otherwise they would have been given here.

THE MANX LANGUAGE.

The Secretary to the Governor has the superintendence of the Census. It is much to be regretted that the language-statistics have always been neglected. There are two churches where, once a month, the service is in Manx. As Man is seventeen miles distant from Scotland, twenty-eight miles from England, and twenty-eight miles from Ireland, the island geographically belongs to Scotland. It is likely that the first inhabitants of Man went to it from Scotland.

Man received its name from Mainus, a son of Fergus the First, who ascended the throne of Scotland 290 B.C. The island belonged to Scotland from at least 290 B.C. to A.D. 395, or 685 years. Also from the year 581 to 611, or thirty years. Also from the year 1266 to 1344, or seventy-eight years. These three periods make 793 years. In 1603, James VI. of Scotland became also king of England : previous to 1603, Man for 793 years belonged to Scotland. The southern isles of the Hebrides were put in a group with Man, and hence arose the name Sodor and Man. (There is not only an inaccuracy, but something more, in the Bishop of Man being styled of Sodor.) For some time the Duke of Athol (by marriage with one of the Stanley family, the family of the Earl of Derby) was titular King of Man. As Europe was peopled from east to west, perhaps emigrants from Scotland passed over to Man, and thence to Ireland. Portpatrick, in Scotland, is only twenty-two miles distant from Ireland.

Registrar-General, William Donelly, Esq.
Superintendent of Medical Statistics, William M. Burke, Esq.
— Wilkie, Esq., Secretary to the Census Commissioners.

NUMBER OF THE IRISH-SPEAKING POPULATION.

Province of	In 1851.			In 1861.			Proportion per cent. of Persons speaking Irish to the whole Population.	
	Who spoke Irish only.	Who spoke Irish & English.	Total Persons speaking Irish.	Who spoke Irish only.	Who spoke Irish & English.	Total Persons speaking Irish.	In 1851.	In 1861.
Leinster ...	200	58,976	59,176	238	35,466	35,704	3·5	2·5
Ulster	146,336	669,449	815,785	62,039	483,492	545,531	43·9	36·3
Munster ...	35,783	100,693	136,476	23,180	91,639	114,819	6·8	6·0
Connaught.	137,283	375,566	512,849	77,818	331,664	409,482	50·8	44·9
Whole of Ireland...	319,602	1,204,684	1,524,286	163,275	942,261	1,105,536	23·3	19·1

The reader will observe that in ten years, the percentage of Irish-speaking persons to the whole population fell from twenty-three to nineteen. The year 1851 was the first time that the Irish-language statistics were taken. The results for 1871 have not yet (May, 1872) been published, otherwise they would have been given here. The intelligent way in which, since 1851, the Irish Census has been taken deserves the greatest praise, and ought to be imitated by the other three Celtic-speaking parts of the United Kingdom.

ESSAYS AND PAPERS

BY

THOMAS STRATTON,

M.D. of the University of Edinburgh, 1 August, 1837;
Licentiate of the Royal College of Surgeons of Edinburgh, 18 April, 1837;
Staff-Surgeon, Royal Navy, 13 May, 1859;
Deputy Inspector-General of Hospitals and Fleets, 5 June, 1867.

PUBLISHED IN THE EDINBURGH MEDICAL & SURGICAL JOURNAL.

14. On Tertian Intermittent Fever. *April*, 1845.
15. Notice of an Epidemic of Scarlet Fever and Scarlet Sore Throat which prevailed in 1843-44. *April*, 1845.
16. On Malarial Fevers, as observed in Canada from 1838 to 1845. Part I. On Malarial Continued Fever. *July*, 1845.
17. Case of Gun-shot Wound, and Excision of the Head of the Humerus : the result a useful Arm. *January*, 1846.
18. On Malarial Fevers, as observed in Canada from 1838 to 1846. Part II. Analysis of Repeated Attacks in the same Individual. *July*, 1846.
19. Meteorological Observations in Canada in 1843 and 1844. *January*, 1847.
20. Meteorological Observations in Canada in 1845. *July*, 1847.
21. On the Comparative Deodorizing Powers of the Disinfecting Fluids of Sir William Burnett and of Mr. Ledoyen. *January*, 1843.
22. Meteorological Observations in Canada in 1846 and 1847. *January*, 1848.
23. Remarks on the Sickness and Mortality among the Emigrants to Canada in 1847, and Suggestions for an improved Method of Regulating Future Emigration. (Ten pages.) *July*, 1848.
24. Remarks on Antiseption, Deodorization, and Disinfection, and on Sir William Burnett's Disinfecting Fluid, the Solution of the Chloride of Zinc. (Eleven pages.) *October*, 1848.
25. Cases of Recovery from Poisoning with Chloride of Zinc, and the Proposal of an Antidote for this Poison: (The Antidote is Carbonate of Soda, or Carbonate of Potash, or Soap.) *October*, 1848.
26. Additional Notes on the Sickness and Mortality among the Emigrants to Canada in 1847. *January*, 1849.
27. Contribution to an Account of the Diseases of the North American Indians. *April*, 1849.
28. On the Comparative Therapeutic Powers of Quinine and Bebeerine. *October*, 1849.
29. Medical Remarks on Emigrant Ships to North America. *January*, 1850.
30. History of the Epidemic Cholera in Chatham and Rochester in 1849. (Forty-four pages.) *April*, 1851.
31. Notice of the Chatham and Rochester Leper Hospital. *July*, 1851.
32. On the British Naval Medical Department, and that of the United States. *January*, 1852.

33. On the Employment of a Long, Flexible Stethoscope for Self-auscultation. *January,* 1852.
34. On the Mortality in the Medical Department of the Navy for the Ten Years ending in 1851. *January,* 1853.
35. Meteorological Observations in Prince-Edward Island in 1851. *April,* 1853.
36. Statistics of Shipwreck-Mortality in the British Navy for Fifty-seven Years. *July,* 1853.
37. On Poisoning with Chloride of Zinc, and on a lately-published Case thereof; with Notes of Eight Cases. *July,* 1854.
38. On the Rate of Mortality in the Medical Department of the Navy for the Nine Years ending in 1860. *March,* 1861.
39. On the Rate of Mortality in the Medical Department of the Navy for the Ten Years ending in December, 1870. *March,* 1871.

Likewise other Communications in the *Numbers* for *July,* 1843; *January,* 1849; *April,* 1850; and *April,* 1852.

OF THE ABOVE PAPERS:—

No. 17 appeared also in the Montreal *British American Medical Journal,* 1846.

No. 21 appeared also in the *British American Medical Journal,* 1848.

No. 23 appeared also in the *British American Medical Journal,* April, 1848. Also in pamphlet-form; eighteen pages; fifty copies printed. This Paper was inserted at full-length in three Montreal newspapers, of 7th and 8th April, 1848, and in *Simmonds' Colonial Magazine* (London), June, 1848.

No. 24 appeared also in the *British American Medical Journal,* June, 1848. Also in pamphlet-form; sixteen pages; one hundred copies printed.

No. 25 appeared also in the *British American Medical Journal,* December, 1848.

No. 30 appeared also in pamphlet-form; forty-four pages; one hundred copies printed.

Bibliotheca Scoto-Celtica; or, an Account of all the Books that have been printed in the Gaelic Language. By John Reid. (Glasgow, 1832. Pp. 72 and 178. 12s. It is much to be desired that we had an edition brought down to the present time.

Ossian's Poems. Translated by James Macpherson. There have been numerous editions; the smaller ones omit the notes. In Macmillan's Magazine, June, 1871, is an article on Ossian by Principal Shairp of St. Andrew's. He believes that the poems are genuine. I believe that they are genuine, of great antiquity, and composed by Ossian.

Fingal; a Poem of Ossian. Translated by James Macpherson, and rendered into Verse by Ewen Cameron. Warrington, 1776. 4to. Pp. 419.

Ossian's Poems in Gaelic, with a Latin Translation by Robert Macfarlan, an Essay by Sir John Sinclair, Bart., and Notes by John Macarthur, LL D. Published by the Highland Society of London. London, 1807. 3 vols., 8vo. 42s.

Some of Ossian's Lesser Poems rendered into Verse, with an Essay by Archibald Macdonald. Liverpool and London, 1805. Pp. 284.

The Highland Society's Report on Ossian. 1805.

Darthula; a Poem of Ossian rendered into Blank Verse by — Burke.

Darthula; a Poem of Ossian translated into Greek by the Hon. and Rev. William Herbert, Dean of Manchester.

Ossian's Remains. Edited by Patrick Macgregor. London, 1841. 12s.

Ossian's Poems in Gaelic, with a metrical translation by the Rev. Archibald Clerk. Edinburgh, 1871. 2 vols., 8vo. 31s. 6d. This beautiful edition owes its publication to the generosity of the Marquis of Bute.

In all these works relating to Ossian, there is in the essays and notes much information respecting Gaelic.

Historical Proofs respecting the Gael of Albyn, and the Highlanders of Scotland. By Colonel James A. Robertson. Second Edition. Edinburgh, 1856. Pp. 642. 6s. This is a most interesting work.

The Gaelic Topography of Scotland. By Colonel James A. Robertson. Edinburgh, 1859. Pp. 544. 7s. 6d. The author deserves well of all Highlanders.

Words and Places. By the Rev. Isaac Taylor, A.M. London, 1864. 2 vols. This admirable work was first seen by me in Jan., 1869.

The Gaelic Language; its Classical Affinities and Distinctive Character. A Lecture by John Stuart Blaikie, Professor of Greek in the University of Edinburgh. Edinburgh: Edmonston & Douglas, 1864. Pp. 32.

A Lecture on the Gaelic Language. By Professor Blaikie. Delivered at Oban, in September, 1870. May be found in the third number of the Gael (1871), a Gaelic monthly magazine (with a supplement in English).

The Gael ; a Gaelic monthly magazine (with a supplement in English). Octavo. The first three numbers were printed in Toronto, Canada; the fourth number in Glasgow. It will in future be printed in Glasgow. For twelve numbers, to all parts of the United Kingdom and North America, 6s. sterling, and 6d. postage; to Australia, New Zealand, &c., 6s., and 1s. postage. Nicolson & Co., 74, Argyle Street, Glasgow. No. 4 is for June, 1872.

Articles on Celtic subjects are to be found in the Dublin University Magazine for October and December, 1869, and January, 1870 ; and in the Broadway for July and August, 1871 (a London monthly magazine, published at 14, York Street, Covent Garden).

Macalpine's Pronouncing Gaelic-English Dictionary. Fifth Edition. Edinburgh, 1866. 5s.

Macalpine's English-Gaelic Dictionary. 5s.
We ought to be very grateful to Mr. Neil Macalpine for his Pronouncing Dictionary. As far as I know, no other Celtic language possesses a pronouncing dictionary. Mr. Macalpine died in 1867 or 1868, in North Perthshire.

The Bible-Student's Concordance. By Aaron Pick, Professor of Hebrew and Chaldee, from the University of Prague. London: Hamilton, Adams, & Co. Printed by Macintosh, London. 1845. Quarto. Pp. 590. 35s. This is a Concordance to the Old Testament only. The alphabetical arrangement is according to the English translation. Each word is followed by its meaning in Hebrew in Hebrew characters, and then in Hebrew in English letters. The work has long been out of print. It is strange that it has not been reprinted.
For the use of this work, and other books relating to Hebrew, I am indebted to the kindness of the Rev. John M. Charlton, M.A., Western College, Mannamead, Plymouth.

A Glossary of Cornish Names. By the Rev. John Bannister, LL.D. London : Williams and Norgate. 1871. Pp. 212. 12s.

The Nomenclature of Cornwall. By Dr. Bannister. (*In preparation.*)
Dr. Bannister deserves great praise for the attention he gives to the remains of the Celtic of Cornwall.

The Physical History of Mankind. By James Cowles Prichard, M.D. London, 1837. 3 vols., 8vo.

Obermüller's German-Celtic Historical and Geographical Dictionary; or, Deutsch-Keltisches Wörterbuch. Leipzig : Ludwig Denicke. London : Williams and Norgate. 1867.

Stuart Glennie's Arthurian Localities in Scotland. London : Macmillan. 1869. 7s. 6d. (Also see Macmillan's Magazine, Dec., 1867.)

Edmunds' Names of Places in England and Wales. New Edition. London, 1872. 6s.

Joyce's Irish Names of Places. Third Edition. Dublin, 1871. 7s. 6d.
On the Study of Celtic Literature. By Matthew Arnold. 1867. 8s. 6d.
  The last five works I have not yet had an opportunity of seeing.
  Messrs. Maclachlan and Stewart, South Bridge, Edinburgh,
  issue a list of Gaelic Books, Grammars, Dictionaries, and works
  relating to Gaelic literature; and to this list I beg to refer any
  young student of the old language of Scotland.

THE GRAMPIAN CLUB (OF LONDON)

Was founded in the autumn of 1868, for the purpose of printing
manuscripts and works relating to Scottish literature, history, and
antiquities. The works issued have been Dr. Rogers' *Scotland, Social
and Domestic;* Mr. Oliphant's *Jacobite Lairds of Gask;* Dr. Rogers'
Scottish Monuments (first volume). In April, 1872, each member
received as a gift from the Marquis of Bute (a member of the G. C.)
the *Cartulary of Cambuskenneth Abbey.* This is a splendid quarto of
438 pages, with many engravings.
  The Rev. Charles Rogers, LL.D., is the honorary secretary. The
honorary treasurer is Alfred Gliddon, Esq., City Bank, 159, Tottenham-
Court Road, London. The expenses are limited to postages and
stationery. There is no entry-money. One guinea is the yearly
payment, due in January. In April, 1872, the number of members
was two hundred and eight. Of course, the more members a Printing
Club has, the more it is able to publish. There is no limit to the
number of members. As one of them, I take this opportunity of
helping to make known the excellent objects the Club has in view.

OMITTED.

In Page 56, third line from the foot.
  For Acha, *a plain,* read Acha, *a field, a plain, a meadow:* hence Low-
land-Scotch haugh, level ground on a river-side, as the Haugh of
Meiklour; the *gh* sounded like *ch* in loch.

W. Brendon and Son, Printers, Plymouth.

LIST OF GAELIC BOOKS

And Works on the Highlands

PUBLISHED AND SOLD BY

MACLACHLAN & STEWART,

BOOKSELLERS TO THE UNIVERSITY,

64 SOUTH BRIDGE, EDINBURGH.

A liberal discount allowed on orders for exportation
or for private circulation.

---

	s.	*d.*
GAELIC DICTIONARIES.		
Armstrong's Gaelic Dictionary, 4to, *half calf*, ...	30	0
Highland Society's Gaelic Dictionary, 2 vols. 4to, *bds.*	70	0
M'Alpine's Gaelic and English Pronouncing Dictionary, with Grammar, 12mo, *cloth*,	9	0
... Ditto ditto *half bound calf*,	10	6
... Gaelic and English, separately, *cloth*, ...	5	0
... English and Gaelic, separately, *cloth*, ...	5	0
M'Leod and Dewar's Gaelic Dictionary, 8vo, *cloth*,	10	6

Alleine's Saint's Pocket-Book, *cloth*, 1s. *sewed*,	0	6
... Alarm, 18mo, *cloth*, ...	1	6
Almanac for 1872, in Gaelic, ...	0	3
Assurance of Salvation, 18mo, *sewed*, ...	0	6
Baxter's Call to the Unconverted, 18mo, *cloth*, ...	1	6
... Saint's Rest, translated by Rev. J. Forbes,	2	6
Beith's Catechism on Baptism, 18mo, *sewed* ...	0	1
Bible in Gaelic, 8vo, *strongly bound in calf*, ...	7	6
Do. Quarto edition of 1826, *calf*, ...	25	0
Boston's Fourfold State, 12mo, *cloth*, ...	4	0
Bonar's (Rev. Dr H.) Christ is All, 18mo, *sewed*,	0	3
Buchannan (Dugald) of Rannoch's Life and Conversion, with his Hymns, 18mo, *cloth*, ...	2	0
... The Hymns, separately, 18mo, *sewed*, ...	0	3

---

64 South Bridge, Edinburgh.

	s.	d.
Bunyan's Come and Welcome, 18mo, *cloth*, ...	2	0
... World to Come, or Visions from Hell, *cloth*,	1	6
... Grace Abounding, 18mo, *cloth*, ...	2	0
... Pilgrim's Progress, *(three parts) cloth*, ...	2	6
... Do. do. *(two parts)* 12mo, 1840,	2	0
... Water of Life, 18mo, *cloth*, ...	1	0
... Sighs from Hell, 18mo, *cloth*, ...	2	0
... Heavenly Footman, 18mo, *cloth*, ...	1	0
... Holy War, 18mo, *cloth*, ...	2	6
Burder's Village Sermons, 18mo, *cloth*, ...	1	6
Campbell (Donald) on the Language, Poetry, and		
Music of the Highland Clans, *with Music*,	7	6
Catechism, Shorter, 1d. Gaelic and English,	0	2
... Mother's, 1d. Gaelic and English,	0	2
... Shorter, with Proofs, ...	0	1½
... Brown's Shorter, for Young Children,	0	1
Confession of Faith, fcap. 8vo, *cloth*, ...	2	6
Dewar's (Rev. Dr.) The Gaelic Preacher, 8vo, ...	0	4
Doctrine and Manner of the Church of Rome, ...	0	3
Doddridge's Rise and Progress, 12mo, *cloth*, ...	3	0
Dyer's Christ's Famous Titles, 18mo, *cloth*, ...	2	6
Earle's Sacramental Exercises, 18mo, *cloth*, ...	1	6
Edwards' (Rev. Jonathan) Sermon, *sewed*, ...	0	2
English Poems, with Gaelic Translations, arranged		
on opposite pages, 12mo, *cloth*, ...	3	6
Farquharson's (A.) Address to Highlanders respecting		
their Native Gaelic (in English), 8vo, *sewed*,	0	6
Finlayson (Rev. R.) Brief Sketch of the Life of,		
by Rev. J. Macpherson, 18mo, *cloth*, ...	1	0
Flavel's Token for Mourners, 18mo, *cloth*, ...	1	0
Forbes' (Rev. J.) Gaelic Grammar, 12mo, 4s. for	2	6
... Baptism and the Lord's Supper, ...	0	4
... An Lochran : Dialogues regarding the Church,	0	6
... Long Gheal : The White Ship ; a Spiritual Poem,	0	4
Gaelic First Book, 18mo, 2d.; Second do. ...	0	4
Gaelic Spelling-Book, 18mo, *cloth*, ...	0	6
Gaelic Tracts, 50 different kinds, *sorted*, for ...	2	6 ·

64 South Bridge, Edinburgh.

	s.	*d.*
Grant's (Rev. Peter) Hymns, 18mo, *cloth*, ...	1	6
Guthrie's Christian's Great Interest, 18mo, *cloth*,	2	0
Hall's (Newman) Come to Jesus, ...	0	6
Harp of Caledonia, Gaelic Songs, 32mo, *sewed*,	0	3
History of Animals Named in the Bible, ...	0	6
History of Prince Charles, fcap. 8vo, *cloth*, ...	3	0
itto ditto *cheap edition, sewed*, ...	1	6
Jacobite Songs, with Portrait of Prince Charles,	0	9
James' Anxious Enquirer, 12mo, *sewed*, ...	1	0
Joseph, Life of, by Macfarlane, 18mo, *cloth*, ...	1	6
Joseph, History of, 18mo, *sewed*, ...	0	4
Laoidhean Eadar-Theangaichte o'n Bheurla,12mo. *cl.*	0	6
Lessons on the Shorter Catechism and the Holy		
Scriptures, by Forbes, 18mo, ...	0	4
M'Callum's History of the Church of Christ, 8vo,	4	0
... The Catholic or Universal Church, ...	0	6
Maccoll's Mountain Minstrel, Clarsach Nam Beann,		
18mo, *cloth*, 1s. 6d. The same, English, ...	2	6
Macdonald's (Rev. Dr) Gaelic Poems, 18mo, *cloth*,	2	6
... Hymns, 18mo, *sewed*, ...	0	2
M'Farlane's Manual of Devotion, 12mo, *bound*,	2	0
M'Gregor's (Rev. Dr) Gaelic Poems, 18mo, *cloth*,	0	8
M'Intyre's (Duncan Ban) Poems and Songs, 18mo,	2	0
M'Intyre (Rev. D.) on the Antiquity of the Gaelic		
Language (in English), ...	1	6
Mackay's (Rob Donn) Songs and Poems, 18mo,	2	6
Mackenzie's (A.) History of Scotland, Eachdraidh		
na H-Alba, 12mo, *cloth*, ...	3	6
Mackenzie's Beauties of Gaelic Poetry, rl. 8vo. ...	12	0
... Gaelic Melodist, 32mo, ...	0	4
Macleod, Rev. Dr., Sermon on the Life of the late,		
by Rev. John Darroch, 8vo, *sewed*, 1s. for	0	6
M'Lauchlan's (Rev. Dr) Celtic Gleanings, or		
Notices of the History and Literature of the		
Scottish Gael (in English), fcap, 8vo, *cloth*,	2	6
M'Naughton (Peter) on the Authenticity of the		
Poems of Ossian (in English), 8vo, ...	0	6

	s.	d.
Macpherson's " Duanaire," a New Collection of Songs, &c., *never before published*, 18mo, *cl.*	2	0
Menzies' Collection of Gaelic Songs, 8vo, *cloth*,	6	0
Mountain Songster, Collection of Original and Selected Gaelic Songs, *sewed*, 6d ; *per dozen*,	4	6
Munro's Gaelic Grammar, 18mo, *bound*, ...	4	0
... Gaelic Primer and Vocabulary, 12mo, ...	2	0
... Selection of Gaelic Songs, 32mo, ...	0	4
Ossian's Poems, revised by Dr M'Lauchlan, *cloth*,	3	0
Peden's Two Sermons and Letters, 18mo, *sewed*,	0	6
Philipps' Seven Common Faults, translated by Rev. H. Maccoll. 12mo, ...	1	6
Prayers and Admonitions, (series of six, large type,) in packets of 2 dozen, *sorted*, ...	0	6
Psalm Book, (General Assembly's Version), large type, 18mo, *bound*, ...	2	6
Do. do. 18mo, *cloth*, ...	1	0
Do. Smith's or Ross's, large type, 18mo, *bd.*	2	0
Do. Gaelic and English, on one page, ...	1	6
Ross's Shorter Catechism, 1d ; *per dozen*,	0	9
Ross's (William) Gaelic Songs, 18mo, *cloth*, ...	1	6
Sinner's (The) Friend, 12mo, *sewed*, ...	0	3
Sixteen Short Sermons, 12mo, *sewed*, ...	0	2
Stewart's Gaelic Grammar, 8vo, *cloth*, ...	4	0
Stratton on the Celtic Origin of Greek and Latin, *cl.*	2	6
Sum of Saving Knowledge, 12mo, *sewed*	0	4
Thomson's (Dr) Sacramental Catechism, 18mo, *sewed*,	0	2
Watts' Divine Songs, with Cuts, ...	0	2
Whitfield's Sermons, 18mo, *sewed*, ...	1	0
Willison's Sacramental Catechism, 12mo, *sewed*,	0	8
New Testament for Schools, 12mo, *bound*, ...	1	0
Job to Ecclesiastes, (for the use of Schools), ...	0	2
Proverbs of Solomon, do. do. ...	0	2

BIBLES, TESTAMENTS, AND PSALM BOOKS

AT VARIOUS PRICES.

64 South Bridge, Edinburgh.

www.ingramcontent.com/pod-product-compliance
Lightning Source LLC
Chambersburg PA
CBHW020236090426
42735CB00010B/1724